Adolescent Depression

Adolescent Depression

✦

Outside/In

Kathleen Keena, MA, LPC, LADC

iUniverse, Inc.
New York Lincoln Shanghai

Adolescent Depression
Outside/In

iUniverse books may be ordered through booksellers or by contacting:

iUniverse
2021 Pine Lake Road, Suite 100
Lincoln, NE 68512
www.iuniverse.com
1-800-Authors (1-800-288-4677)

ISBN-13: 978-0-595-35993-6 (pbk)
ISBN-13: 978-0-595-80444-3 (ebk)
ISBN-10: 0-595-35993-0 (pbk)
ISBN-10: 0-595-80444-6 (ebk)

Printed in the United States of America

Contents

Acknowledgments

To depressed adolescents and the people who love them.
Thanks to Clark Bowlen, my husband, for his extensive technical assistance and emotional support throughout this process.
Dedicated with special thanks, love, gratitude, and humility to Shirley Allen, my mentor, for believing in me.

1

Adolescent Depression: Why This Book?

I spent my young adulthood exploring the landscape of depression. I was a plane out of fuel, circling, and the subsequent crash was inevitable. From my early teens to late twenties, I alienated others with snap judgments, erratic behavior, and sudden outrage. I knew I was different from my classmates. Impulsive and irrational, I was afraid of and for myself. The crash and burn was impossible for me to observe. I can only explain how it felt from within. I did not have the confidence or success my classmates had. By sixteen, the prospect of becoming employed, living on my own, and continuing peer relationships left me terrified. What if I never matured? Would they know? Would my parents know? How would I cope? Then, the inevitable conclusion of depression thundered in my mind: *No one loves you.*

I inadvertently kept records of my descent. I had no intention of sharing, publishing, or even being literally correct. Some writers write to create an alternate reality. I wrote for survival. I wrote to make sense of my fears, failings, logic, and disappointments. The pieces of paper became parachutes to safety preserved on paper scraps, brown bags, napkins, and notebook pages. I read those scraps of paper when I did not know who I was or why I was alive. All of these writings included in this book, with minor editorial changes for clarity, are as I wrote them at the time.

In the summer of 1971, working at the town drugstore, I became friends with an older man. After a few weeks of meeting on the hill behind the store, I slipped through the backyard gate of our small suburban home to go into hiding until we could leave the country to find John Lennon and Yoko Ono. Lennon and Ono were pop culture legends—alienated talented, raw, avant-garde artists. We shared a delusion that they could guide us toward…something better.

Who wouldn't identify with their brilliance and their rage? We traveled from New England to London to join them. However, Apple Records was not expecting us, and the couple had since moved to New York City. The gray rain, puddle-filled sidewalks, misty air, and tiny shops filled with fruit and vegetable baskets helped me believe I was anonymous. However, I was underage, and by then my grandfather had initiated an Interpol search. I wanted to acquire the working papers necessary to remain in London, but I lacked the knowledge and resources to follow through. I returned to the town high school, more of an enigma, barely graduating with my class.

At nineteen, following two years of college, I married a classmate from my acting studies at Hartford Stage. He planned to travel to Los Angeles and become an actor. It sounded good to me. We drove cross-country with a thousand dollars, a battered car, and no idea where we would live or work. Fortunately, the Strasburg Studio of Los Angeles accepted me. Unfortunately, I found it startlingly easy to shift from role to role and more difficult to return to myself. My conscious and subconscious mind would scramble reality with imagination. It was all the same open corridor.

Working in the retail environment provided tenuous grounding. Stocking vitamins and small appliances somewhat stabilized my emotional distress. I also made some friends, and friendship was a safety net, despite my deepening depression. When my husband and I broke up and my best friend moved back to Boston with her daughter, I returned to the East Coast. I was twenty-four.

I continued in retail management, and my emotions remained impaired. I displayed a lack of flexibility with myself and others, had frequent crying episodes at work, and experienced extreme confusion. I began "first generation" antidepressants. The attendant side effects of dry mouth, gastrointestinal distress, and a spaced-out feeling marked the beginning of my healing. I did not expect to live to thirty. I did not expect to be understood. I could not imagine a career, due to my unpredictable and magnified emotional reactions. I carried the guilt of my impulsive disappearances after others had forgiven me. Later, when I began to get better, I finished an undergraduate degree and then two master's degrees with highest honors. I hadn't known or cared about my aptitude. The emotional distraction of my depression was a full-time job. Writing was responsible for my safe landing despite the crushing crash of my deepening depression, and I was fortunate.

In the past decade, I have practiced as a clinician and clinical director. I have observed that adolescents are particularly vulnerable because they have not yet found resources to help make sense of their behavior and, consequently conclude that their suffering is their fault. Since depression is often dormant prior to adolescence, the symptoms may be mistaken for defiance. A depressed adolescent can act irritable and inattentive and be considered delinquent. The depressed adolescent needs counseling to adjust a pessimistic outlook and psychiatric assessment for possible antidepressants, nonaddicting anti-anxiety medication, or sleep aids. Pressuring or morally correcting the adolescent will not help.

This book is written as a bridge between the objective and subjective perspectives of depression to help adolescents understand the phenomenon more fully. For the parents of an adolescent who suffers from depression, an inside view of the disease can help them understand what measures will be most beneficial for their child. This book features my adolescent writings in the hope that they will give a new understanding of adolescent depression and help caretakers find methods of easing the pain for a child.

Each chapter begins with a description, in lay terms, of one aspect of adolescent depression and includes a selection of my poetry and stories to illustrate that aspect. I do not claim to know adolescent clinical depression exhaustively, but I do know adolescent depression experientially. I hope that the dual perspective will help parents and adolescents recognize the illness and seek treatment.

Depression should always be taken seriously. It can be, and is, deadly when a young person despairs of getting better. For all the underachievers staring out classroom windows, for all the distracted, lost young adults who find themselves fearing a compromised future, I urge you to believe that depression is treatable. A supportive circle of family or friends and counseling, education, and psychiatric attention are components of compassionate care. Recovery is possible. You deserve it.

2

Adolescent Depression and Early Childhood Symptoms

OUTSIDE VIEW

Recognizing the symptoms that indicate a predisposition to adolescent depression in a child's early years allows parents to help children develop their strengths and deal with their weaknesses. For example, the acute sensitivity that causes a child to be fearful of noise may also be the basis of musical talent. By encouraging that talent, parents can nurture the ability that will serve as a lifeline for the child in difficult years ahead.

In looking for symptoms that indicate a predisposition to depression in young children, parents should be aware of the wide diversity of normal personality, even in newborns. From birth, children differ in intelligence, endurance, and patterns of behavior. One child is alert, another is hesitant; one child may display agitation from early infancy while another is content to sleep through the night. Symptoms of depression may be found in children without any significant clinical impairment. It is a matter of severity. Children who display a number of these symptoms over time are more likely to be depressed.

My professional observations and personal experience demonstrate a common trait in biological depression: acute sensitivity. Babies who are painfully startled by sounds or do not tolerate minor digestive distress are displaying symptoms of hypersensitivity. Children who are extremely sensitive to sounds, smells, and sights can suffer from sensory overload. Sometimes a sensitive child will be sad, frightened, or angry without obvious cause and will not be comforted by sympathy or distracted by a shift in activity. In preschool years, children may display acute sensitivity that is not purely physical, but social, by shying away from new people and new situations.

Sensitivity may also be shown by intuitive creativity, unusually advanced appreciation for the arts and sciences, or ability in languages, mathematics, or performance. A childhood predisposition to adolescent depression might be his or her ability with imaginary play. Some children may view inanimate objects as alive or may create a special playmate. They develop an interior life and are more likely than other children to play alone. In the company of other children, they interact with less ease. Social awkwardness is common. In the classroom, their concentration may be impaired.

Artistic precociousness, exceptional verbal ability, unusual insight, and original problem solving may be related to adolescent depression. Creativity is not inspired by exterior events but by interior ones. Depression-prone children also display a lack of resiliency in facing challenges and stress. Sensitive children, compared with their peers, have a low tolerance for frustration and may display an intense emotional reaction to any disappointment. They often avoid team sports and competitive games. They do not adapt easily to change and may be slow to advance through progressive stages of independence.

Physical symptoms of a predisposition to depression include a lack of energy, unusual appetite, difficulty sleeping, or prolonged sleep. They may do poorly in school and become increasingly isolated from the social life of their peers.

Although depression is not caused by even the worst kind of childhood experience, the quality of the family life has an important effect on children prone to depression. Harsh words and stern voices are frightening to sensitive children. A further complication is that, since the disease is inherited, one parent or both may also be depressed and almost unable to cope with a "difficult" child.

The best family environment is stable, affirming, and appreciative. The parents try to minimize the sensitive child's limitations by helping her avoid stressful situations. They temper criticism with a mild tone and reassurance of love. They nurture his special abilities by encouraging and, when possible, providing exposure to art classes, music, interpretive movement, literature, drama, and opportunities to explore scientific or mechanical challenges. Bringing up a sensitive child demands much of parents—no one person can fulfill all the physical and emotional needs of a child. Parents have to balance the child's needs against many other claims upon their own time and energy. They should not expect to do everything right.

Early Childhood Symptoms of the Depressed Adolescent

- Looks to caregivers for frequent affirmation

- Displays unusual sensitivity to sounds, harsh lighting, unfamiliar experiences
- Displays uncertainty around other children of the same age
- Displays a rich imagination
- Displays precocious talent in artistic, scientific, mathematical or other specific areas of expertise

ADOLESCENT DEPRESSION AND EARLY CHILDHOOD SYMPTOMS: BRIDGE

This writing stems from painful moments in childhood that demonstrate a lack of resiliency. The pieces are examples of hypersensitivity, solitary play, and the creation of an imaginary world. I wrote "Scales," "Ice Skate Laughter," and "Pre-profound Beatles" during adolescence. "Dolls" was written during my twenties in an attempt to gain a perspective on my childhood experiences that led to adolescent depression.

"Scales" describes the frustration of my isolation as a fifth-grader and retreat from others through piano practice. The repetition of scale practice parallels the helplessness and hopelessness of days filled with flunking gym class in red-and-white-striped short rompers, dreading the time when classmates would choose teams. I didn't blame them for leaving me standing there, but it was a regular reminder of my inadequacy. The predictability of rejection seemed guaranteed.

"Ice Skate Laughter" is also about being outside the circle of the other children, who appeared to enjoy what I found to be torture. I was a large girl, lacking grace, and I was uneasy with physical activities. In addition, I couldn't get girls' ice skates wide enough for my feet, so I could not balance. In fact, I could hardly move in the skates because they were so tight. My winter clothing was pieced together from odds and ends in our family closet, generically available to all of us but with fatal flaws—gloves with holes, scratchy scarves, or coats with missing buttons. My physical discomfort mirrored my emotional discomfort. Some of the worst moments in grade school were spent overhearing laughter and comments in biting, derogatory terms. I was the big, goofy, uncoordinated girl on the playground who could never handle herself gracefully.

"Dolls" is an attempt to reconstruct my childhood isolation by observing myself playing teacher and mother with my dolls, who were my best friends. I loved to give my deserving "students" gentle correction and special attention. In play, I could provide the nonjudgmental focus for my dolls that I craved.

"Pre-profound Beatles" tells of my transition from childhood to adolescence. I believed unquestioningly, or wished to believe, that the baby Jesus could intervene in my life, but serious doubts were surfacing. "Three ungrown brothers under the tree" is a reference to the nursery rhyme "Three Blind Mice," and to the dubious Christmas "present" of reaching adolescence while they remained children.

ADOLESCENT DEPRESSION AND EARLY CHILDHOOD SYMPTOMS: INSIDE VIEW

Scales

When I was playing the scales on the piano
When I was playing the scales
When I was playing the scales on the piano
When I was a little girl
I was the one on the playground hill
who tripped and fell in front of teams
I was the one who couldn't jog
three laps in a row,
who couldn't jump,
who couldn't throw,
who couldn't catch,
who couldn't climb,
and I played those notes
again and again.
Living with fear,
trying to cope.
Hoping to live.

Ice Skate Laughter

Sharp ice skate laughter,
dark nights lit by bonfire,
feet sopping in leaky boots,
from someone else's feet.

These open spaces
at my wrists

where my sleeves were too short
and my mittens too small.

Those obvious wrists: red, hot, chapped,
announcing my ineptness
at winter dress.

Then, my hair;
frizzy, disobedient
molded like a defective helmet
to my skull, daring me to fit in.

The hopelessness of short days;
ears, nose, fingers, toes,
terminally chilled.
The heartless walk to school,
stockings and garters
slicing through my thighs.
Refrigerator raw.

And when I'm grown,
I tell myself,
I will never be
this cold, this wet, this alone
again.

Dolls

At four o'clock, her mother was finally ready to get Daddy. The wind blew softly on the young trees of the new street. Her brothers had been playing on the gig since early afternoon. Ten-year-old Amy had been down in the cellar, teaching her dolls. She had several outstanding dolls who knew all the answers to her questions. One of her dolls, Nancy, was crippled. Her hair was in pipe curls, just like Mom had fixed Amy's hair for church. She gave Nancy a seat in front, near the chalkboard. Everyone in the class received plenty of attention. Of course, they weren't perfect, but that's where she came in.

"Yes. That is correct. You are right again!" she told her student, a tiny rag doll without hair. "Thank you, Sara. You are coming along nicely. You may be seated."

Amy paced the front of the makeshift class holding a yardstick. It was the closest thing she could find to a pointer. She would never hurt anyone's knuckles with it, like the nuns did to Grandma. "I am very pleased with everyone's progress. Please continue the exercise on page fifteen and we will review it together. Questions?" She glanced at her father's workshop clock, at the far end of the cellar. It was almost four now.

"Class, I have a very important teacher's conference to attend. Continue to work until I return." She carefully turned off the cellar lights before bounding up the stairs. Amy's mother was in the kitchen putting supper in the oven. Daddy liked his supper the minute he got in the door. He would be angry if it wasn't ready, then no one would know what to do.

"Mom, can I go with you tonight?" she asked.

Her mother slung her overstuffed purse over her shoulder as she stirred the stew and tested its temperature. Her mother sighed. "I guess so. But I'm leaving right away."

Amy's mother always looked tired. A lot of the time, Amy thought she was mad, too. Amy worked at being very good in case it was her fault. Amy's mother asked her why she was in the cellar so much. She had been athletic as a girl and struggled to understand her daughter, who would rather sit than ride a bike, rather be in the cellar than make new friends. "Why are you so sedentary?" she asked Amy.

That would make a great vocabulary word for her class tomorrow. She would ask her students why they were so sedentary and see if they could come up with an answer. "But what does it mean?" she asked.

"It means you sit around too much!" her mother responded, annoyed. "You act as if you were fifty years old. You're just a young girl. You need to be in the sunshine and meet kids from the neighborhood."

But I like to play school, Amy thought. She would ask her students why they were so sedentary and see if they could come up with an answer.

Amy pulled her clumsy ten-year-old body into the station wagon. She curled up in the back seat, leaning her cheek against the glass window. Her mother dashed into the driver's seat, starting the engine. The car flew out of the driveway as Amy's head flung back with the speed of the departure. Soon they passed the shopping center, church, and her mother was signaling to join the traffic jam heading south. Amy watched the billboards along the highway: Maxwell House (good-to-the-last-drop) coffee, Camel cigarettes, and Mr. Clean. Past the bowling alley landmark the city appeared like a Mecca, buildings silhouetted against the skyline.

Her father worked in the tallest building of them all, the Travelers Tower. He might even work in The Tower, Amy wasn't sure. Someday she would visit him there. It would be like going to see the president, or something.

The car sped past the radio station TIC that broadcasted the morning news Daddy listened to weekdays. Down a shadowed city street, an artery from the route to Main Street, between worn stone architecture, her father was waiting. He wore his steel gray jacket and held his newspaper, folded into thirds. He smelled like Old Spice. He glanced up, signaling her mother to pull to the curb. She did, and quickly slid to the passenger seat as the engine idled. Daddy took the wheel.

"Hi, Dad!" Amy greeted him with a happy smile.

"Oh hi, honey," he answered, without looking at her. Then, addressing her mother, he began a stress-filled litany all the way to their suburban driveway. "Unbelievable pressure to get that contract out…" he started.

"You can only go as fast as the job takes, so it's not worth getting upset over, Alan," her mother comforted, or tried to comfort him.

"Ha! Yeah, tell that to Sanders and see how far that flies!"

"*Oh, Alan!* The red Ford on your left!"

"I saw him!" he retorted.

Yeah! He saw him! Amy thought, knowing her dad was the best driver in the world. Amy drifted into a trance of trust with both parents there. Why were so many people mean to Daddy? If only they would be nicer to him, he would be happy.

"We're going to have a nice supper tonight, so you can relax and enjoy the evening. I'm making the beef stew you like so much."

"My stomach's been acting up again."

"Oh, dear," her mother said in her gentle voice. Amy loved her mother's gentle voice. It reminded her of soft blankets and rocking. Her dolls liked the gentle voice, too. She would be their mother after class if they had a stomachache or anything. She would say, "You are the best little girls in the world," and comfort them. All her dolls were so special.

"Geeze, I'll be glad for vacation this year!" Daddy said, shaking his head. Amy gripped the back of her seat. She reminded herself she was going to be just like Daddy when she grew up. And if they get on my nerves I'll tell them where to go!

So there! Daddy drove a lot faster than Mom did. Amy thought it was about thirty seconds until they pulled into the driveway.

"You sure drive fast, Dad!" Amy said. Her father did not answer.

They piled out of the car. Her father loosened his tie and carefully hung his suit jacket.

"Ginny, is supper ready?" he asked, snapping on the TV in the living room.

"I'll set the table, Mom!" Amy announced.

"Good," her mother answered. "Get the white lace tablecloth out and unload the dishwasher. Call your brothers in and tell Grandpa supper will be ready in five minutes. Hurry!" Her mother's hands were shaking and her voice was several octaves higher than it had been an hour ago.

Amy could hear her brothers laughing from the back yard. Jimmy was correcting the younger two, Tommy and Randy, on the right way to throw a ball. Tommy was five and Randy, four.

"It has to go this way, okay?" Jimmy said, as Tommy looked on, breathing from his mouth, looking permanently confused regardless of the technical lesson. Randy grabbed Tommy's sleeve to take a closer look.

"Got it?" Jimmy demanded, Tommy nodding vigorously. "So do it!" Jimmy ordered, as Tommy fumbled with the ball.

"Hey you guys!" Amy called. "Mom wants you in here for supper, so hurry up."

"Okay," Jimmy replied, hustling his younger brothers by their shoulders to the edge of the screen door. Daddy was watching *Star Trek* as Amy's brothers tumbled in.

"Don't slam the door, you kids!" their father said, angrily, as the screen door slammed behind them. "Jimmy. Take out the trash for your mother. Get those muddy shoes off, Randy!"

"Stupid kid," Tommy said, helping Randy, or trying to help him take his shoes off quickly. Amy rushed over to take Randy's shoes off, then hurried downstairs to call their grandfather for supper.

Her brothers joined their father for *Star Trek*. Everything was so much more exciting when Daddy was home. She wanted to sit with them but knew her mother would need help in the kitchen. Instead, she mentally reviewed the day in school, in case Daddy asked her. She knew if he didn't have so much on his mind he would be happy to talk to her. He was Captain Kirk. The whole house was the *Enterprise*.

"Do you have to have that on so loud?" their mother yelled from the kitchen. Amy looked at Daddy. His eyes were shut and he wasn't watching TV.

"Dad, Dad, don't fall asleep, *Star Trek* is on!"

He jumped a bit, startled. "Right. Amy, go help your mother in the kitchen."

She slunk away, sadly. From the huge living room window she could see the darkening sky. Amy loved the twilight best of all. The mysterious time between the day and the night that seemed to promise everything. It was always right before supper. She had the feeling something wonderful would happen. Maybe tonight it would. Something she could almost feel.

"Supper's ready, Alan," her mother called.

Daddy seated himself at the head of the table with their mother beside him. Grandpa sat at the opposite end. Amy and her brothers were sandwiched between the adults.

"Pass the butter," Daddy said. Then, a flash of anger washed his face as he watched Tommy. "Do *not* spit your meat out on your plate, Tommy!"

"Alan, I'm sorry," their mother replied, in her high-pitched voice that frightened Amy.

"They look like street kids! They're dirty and sweaty and disgusting!" he protested.

Their mother, responding as her brothers froze, sounded annoyed. "They are children, Alan. They get dirty."

But Amy couldn't hear the rest. Suddenly her dolls were crying much too loudly. She thought she better get them, before they became frightened. She ran down the cellar steps, flipping the lights on quickly. Nancy's beautiful hair was pushed to the side and Amy couldn't even see her face. Sarah had a stomachache and Sally had spiked a fever. They were all crying and Amy scooped them up in her lap, hugging each one tightly.

"Don't cry, little babies. You are all the best little girls in all the world." She rocked them back and forth. "Do you know how much your mommy loves you?" They all needed so much attention.

It was eight o'clock before her grandfather came down the cellar stairs to find her. She was curled up with her dolls, asleep. Gently, he unglued their plastic arms from her hands, guiding the girl to her feet and up the stairs.

Pre-profound Beatles #1

Pre-profound Beatles
need somebody
not just anybody.

Three ungrown brothers
under the tree.

That year I received
awkward adolescence:
newly full breasts,
round hips,
hidden by giant shirts
and flowered pants,
terminally tight.
Praying to the baby Jesus,
Mary and Joseph
and the Wise Men
to help her stop growing.
Such a big, big girl.

Pre-profound Beatles #2

1966 to forever
Ancient archetypes
branded into my brain
like a convict's number
seared to skin.
This loop of images
endlessly rolling.

The elementary school walk
past the abandoned dairy house,
that crazy old guy

who always sat
on his front steps, grinning.
Then, years later
the radio station transmitter tower,
the tiny dark room
I never should have entered.
A broken loop.

That orange Volkswagen bus
driving through town,
with me, underground.

Six AM radio
smooth talk from a velvet voice.
Hey there, lonely girl.

3

Adolescent Depression and Symptoms

OUTSIDE VIEW

If a child's depression has remained undetected until he or she reaches adolescence, the illness is more difficult to identify because the physical and hormonal changes of adolescence can produce symptoms that are easily confused with symptoms of genetic depression. It is normal for adolescents to have sudden shifts in mood as they alternately stretch toward independence and retreat into the safety of childhood. One day they may angrily rebel against parental rules and the next meekly ask for guidance. As they search for their own identity, they may try on different roles. An introverted child may become an active, outgoing teen. As adolescents seek self-direction, they are likely to question their parents' values, especially in our present culture of extreme peer pressure, which grants or withholds social status on the basis of fads and behavior.

Although normal adolescent behavior may seem to have some similarity to mental illness, the symptoms of adolescent depression are more severe and long-lasting. Sleeping patterns change with adolescence, but it is not typical for a teen to sleep all weekend. Types of friends may shift, but it is not typical for a teen to consistently prefer isolation.

Adolescent Depression Symptoms

- Displays frequent boredom, irritability
- Demonstrates low energy
- Displays social awkwardness
- Experiences unexplained periods of sadness, weeping

17

- Displays poor eating habits
- Experiences erratic sleep
- Displays poor judgment

Depressed adolescents typically have little tolerance for others, anger easily, avoid peer interaction, and see themselves as different from others and not subject to the same standards of behavior. Such attitudes can be irritating to parents, but they are more harmful to the victims of depression. This insidious condition causes them to consistently underestimate their aptitudes, attractiveness, competence, and personal value. Incidents that others take in stride can cause them to despair. They blame events for their dark moods.

Because depression causes acute suffering and can lead to injury or death through risky behaviors or suicide, a child who has these symptoms should see a professional therapist for diagnosis and treatment. Recognizing the condition as a treatable illness is the first step in the climb out of despair. Cognitive therapy, which examines the irrational beliefs behind low self-esteem, can challenge despairing assumptions. Behavioral therapy helps deal with overwhelming events by breaking them down into small, manageable components. Assisted by education in developing coping skills and destigmatizing depression, and with the help of a trusted therapist, mood swings and anxiety decrease. We are, fortunately, in a time of medication management that can chemically alter the brain's perception of well-being and allow insight-oriented therapy to begin.

ADOLESCENT DEPRESSION AND SYMPTOMS: BRIDGE

The adolescent internal perspective begins with "What Do They Call It?" a collection of voices namelessly involved in the antiseptic diagnosis of one adolescent's depression. The voices include material from a medical chart written by a psychiatrist who failed to provide the compassion needed to identify the depressed teenager's fractured self-esteem. The adolescent speaks about herself in third person, describing the destructive behaviors she has engaged in. She is looking for safety but has made damaging choices trying to get there. The purpose of this material is to show the gap between compassion and sterile observation, and to suggest that emotional despair will deepen as depression progresses.

"Windows" is a retrospective of the dreamlike floating that I often experienced in my room as a teenager. One part of me was on the way out of the window, the other part stayed inside. The windows alternately opened and closed, both freeing and protecting my spirit. The breeze moved through the room, softly reaching the shades and bringing breath to the space.

I wrote "Coffee Bean One" and "Coffee Bean Two" when I was seventeen. I had run away from my home, a small New England town, with an older man who befriended me. I was in hiding for several months before we went to London, England. I did not have the insight to see the long-term effects my disappearance would have on my family. Depression had convinced me that not only did no one love me, but also that I was unworthy of love. The first poem is about identity and self-deception. It was written out of my need to search for honesty, including the self-honesty to face my fears. Before that time, I had run as fast as I could from threatening situations.

I wrote "Coffee Bean Two" to my father. Feeling unloved is a symptom of depression, which produces a state of suspended emotion and a lack of receptivity to the emotions of others. Dad was seriously compromised by depression and unprepared to perceive or respond to mine. His mother was depressed, consequently, it must have been too close. It disturbed him to see me depressed. I now think he was seeing in me what he found unacceptable in himself.

I wrote "Crying Not to Cry" at our family kitchen table. This poem illustrates my frustration at expressing to others how unwell I felt. I saw myself crying for myself, because I could not stop crying. The sea was the only place big enough to absorb my tears. I thought I would become part of the sea.

I modeled "Movement One" after the first movement of a classical sonata. I had been studying piano for years and was working on a Mozart sonata. Every stanza in Mozart is tight, crisp, and precise. The poem describes the similarity between the predictability of a sonata to the expectations implied in relationships. "I but You," written at the same time, is an intentionally fragmented poem. Like my life, it could be read up and down, sideways and across—all reflecting my chaotic state of mind. "The Iron Shadow" is my description of the monster—depression—that had taken control of my life.

In contrast to these poems, I wrote "What Do You Do with Your Anger?" after I was first treated for depression. I had spent my energy holding down my anger and directing it at myself. Gradually, with the help of a wonderful feminist therapist, I recognized that I might not deserve mistreatment. I was allowing myself to be battered until I recognized the open door in front of me. I was twenty-eight. Recovery had begun after fourteen years of hopelessness. I am so grateful every day that I made it into treatment. Emotionally, I was still an adolescent. My coping skills were anemic. I had to go back to learn how to handle situations and life stages that others my age had moved through.

I wrote "High School Years" retrospectively. It is a kinder look at my depression than I had at the time. I now recognize that my friends and I were all in the same sinking boat. All of us were artists. We were suffering from depression, many of us suicidal. None of us knew what the feeling was called. We found each other as nomads, and we became alive in "The Place That Is No Place." The blackness of death beckoned to us, seductively. Some of us fell in love with death. Depression is a trickster and says there is no possibility of problem solving your way out of difficulty. Hopelessness is a component of depression.

"Somewhere on Earth" is ostensibly about living in another place, or planet, where people would be friendlier, kinder, and better nonjudgmental listeners. It is another variation of my longing to be elsewhere. The world was so searing for me, for a time, I thought I was an alien. "Normal" describes my first psychiatric assessment. I was seventeen. As a teenager, I had asked my mother for psychiatric help and felt betrayed when my visit turned into a trivializing of my symptoms. Young people are least equipped to deal with such encounters because they have not yet developed problem-solving skills or a tolerance for frustration. Neither do they have the energy to follow through with care on their own behalf. Depression told me life would never get better. I did not visit a psychiatrist for another ten years, although I very much needed intervention. I had been sufficiently intimidated by that one visit to believe psychiatrists couldn't identify depression when they saw it, so why bother? Today I know if a doctor minimizes or ignores symptoms of depression, another doctor is needed. Listening and understanding are my first requirements. There are resources listed at the end of this book specifically for depressed teens.

"Mending the Fiber" describes the arrested development that occurs with depression. Similar to drug addiction, depression causes one's view of oneself to become askew. In my own experience, my high school classmates were assuming adult roles, while I had missed appropriate socialization with my peers, including successful acceptance of self-responsibility. I remained a teenager until age twenty-eight. Until that time, I functioned marginally.

ADOLESCENT DEPRESSION AND SYMPTOMS: INSIDE VIEW

What Do They Call It?

(The Doctor's Chart)
Adolescent, female
DOB 2/17/54

Medical Record Number: #0000
Gender, age, race, prior diagnosis (if any): female adolescent, well-nourished Caucasian, no prior mental health history reported.

Diagnostic Impression: Manic Depression, most recent episode, mixed, (histrionic features).

Self-report of:
Grades plummeting. Dangerous places—places that would not care whether she was fourteen years old. Older men. Attention. Someone to listen. She would have denied exploitation as the price. Someone quiet enough to hear her, see her, hold her. An even trade. It wasn't as if anyone forced her into this. And she wasn't using drugs. And she wasn't drinking, like some of the other kids. But her judgment floated away. The strong, capable girl who took charge of the younger ones now ventured into darkness without expectation. Just the chance to talk to anyone who wasn't giddy, childish, naive. Any person who might understand. Feeling ageless. Disembodied.

Windows

> Orange wildcat turntable spins.
> Lennon's voice pleads
> Mother! You had me.
> I never had you.
>
> Summer breeze shifts through
> open screens,

powder soft air.
Cotton curtains billow,
tattered shades flap
against sills.

The room,
breathing with the wind,
the shades,
the rhythm of the song,
splitting the emptiness with longing.
Raw, unmodulated pain
pours from
the wildcat turntable.
The silent girl,
dragging her past
like extra eyes
looks out the window,
down the deserted street,
seeing storm clouds.

Coffee Bean One

You are walking with your head bent,
you are walking with your head reaching the sky.
You see reflections on the sidewalks of the sky,
you see reflections in the sky of the sidewalks.
And everything you see
is a reflection of you.
It is dark.

You are a slave and how is a slave
to know freedom?
You must talk to someone who understands but

how can you
when you don't.

I go out to people
but I refuse to bring them in,
I go into people
but refuse to bring them out.
I go out to myself
but refuse to bring me in.
I go into myself
but I refuse to bring me out.

I don't want to see the honesty.
I don't want to give the honesty.
I don't want to recognize the honesty.
But I do.
I lie. I die in lying.
I can't stand to see it.

Coffee Bean Two

Alone,
must I stay.
Within,
must I be.
Afraid,
must I exist
lonely, frightened inside.

You speak to me of love.
Violent, passionate,
all encompassing,
yet
gentle, soft
as spring sunshine.

And as you speak, I feel,
for an instant,
moving within me,
your peace.

And then you go away.

I have touched and felt and seen
but the warmth has frozen hard
like some lost, forgotten dream.
But I remember.

Crying Not to Cry

Burning burned weeping
burned burning weeping
lost soul searching
aches of negative
and all about me
empty laughter.

A blind eye
absurdly blurred with wetness
burning burning weeping
burned burned tears
crying only
not to cry
anymore.

Movement One

When truth and lies seem one the same,
we walk into a hollow cave.

There, behind the shriveled remains
we look for love. A word.

When I was seventeen and green,
I did not know, then, no
that love and despair are one the same.
Cry not/ask not/I love.

Only intrigue, the memory,
God and Goddess meet.
And clasping hands, they freeze to stone.
Then, like the legend,
they turn gold.

I but You

i   but you

      and i   come
      alone

help   but you

      and i   weeping
      wanting

you   but you

      and i   strong
      hope

help   but you

      and i   doubt
      fall

                     but i

me

      and you

The Iron Shadow

Depression slinks and sulks
a coward,
down the corridor,
waiting to devour me.

I am watching, waiting, too.
You can't have me this time!
I scream into dense, seamless air.

Depression's silence
is as vast as space.
Depression calls me a hypocrite.
I know I am alone.

What Do You Do with Your Anger?

What do you do with your anger?
When it hurts too much,
when tears can't be swallowed,
do you choke,
do you suffocate,
do you stuff yourself with chocolate,
do you blame,
do you scream,
do you just go away?
I went away.
I went away and stuffed it down with smiles.
I stayed good, after all
I must have been wrong.
Must have wanted too much.
Must have felt too much.
I must have needed too much.

I must have. It was me.

I am not sorry this time, however.

Not sorry for my anger.

Not sorry I can feel.

And I felt what you said.

And it's time that I said, "Take it back!"

Take back this stuff you tried to stick me with.

It's worth nothing to me.

This guilt stuff, this "inadequate" bullshit,

this "less than" garbage.

I'll take myself whole, thank you.

Anger and all.

High School Years

My high school years were full of alienation, pain, and an endless, undiagnosed depression. I was drawn to similarly compromised classmates. We shadowed one another from year to year in high-honors English classes, probably some of the few teenagers who found solace in the writing of Sylvia Plath, T. S. Elliot, and Ann Sexton more than in the music of Led Zeppelin. Although "Stairway to Heaven" was arrestingly accessible in its seductive, mysteriously tinged promise of redemption within damnation. If you've never been depressed enough to understand this, imagine the last seconds of a dive, between the jump and the slap of water against your body; it is only comforting in its finiteness. Or, think of a stairway. A stairway has a specific amount of stairs. Depression, however, has no finite amount of stairs. It was more like an elevator that took us underground within ourselves, a nonspecific darkness intermittently lit by friendships. But when the darkness would take hold of us, it was impossible to predict whether that person would ever surface.

One friend was hospitalized and, as we later learned, given the antipsychotic medication Thorazine. One day he was just gone, and no one at school or at his home would explain. Several of us ran away, indiscriminately assuming our judgment was sound. We all took stupid risks with unsafe people due either to a lack of reality-based thinking or an impulsive desire toward self-destruction. Or maybe it was both.

We had a weird sort of notoriety. In school, the euphemism for depression was "really smart." If someone said you were really smart, she meant you were really different, difficult, and isolated. It probably meant you did not know how to dress or relate socially. It meant you never went steady, because any normal kid would have no interest or ability to begin a friendship with you. A lot of us befriended teachers who seemed more like contemporaries. Some of those teachers directed us to art schools, some to theater or writing. Some of us trusted no one, and many of us experimented with marijuana, LSD, and alcohol as a way to cope. Sure, every kid goes through some of this. But we lived there.

The Place That Is No Place

Waiting to gobble me up with self-hate, unworthiness, and that booming voice promising nothing would ever get better, hollow and bottomless: a place that is no place, a complete lack of reference. Nothing to measure against. Voices amplify and especially laughter: loud, disturbing, shattering like glass smashed over my head. The brittle glass laughter reminded me that I was not part of the same life others lived. What could be joyful about life? Why were people even bothering to communicate with one another? After all, life was meaningless.

And then, the sudden glances in my direction to disapprove of my pain. Then more carnivorous laughter. Laughter that was red and bright and above the ground. Laughter that had never seen the darkness…or pretended not to see it because it was more convenient to miss.

Somewhere on Earth

> Somewhere on earth
> someone is holding someone and
> for the first time feels a surge of love,
> as if it were something new.
>
> Somewhere on earth, right now,
> someone is reaching a hand
> to a lover's face,
> believing it will never be the same

from this moment on.
But not me, not here, not now.

Somewhere, someone is satisfied.
It is the perfect year for putting
things together.
But not me, not here, not now.

Somewhere on earth,
all is forgiven.
A woman has mastered the balance
of centered living.
And it is so good to be alive.
But not me, not here, not now.

Normal

So that's how it was. Despite the countless times she tried to tell her mother just how bad she felt, her overworked mother's ensuing panic for "professional help" propelled her mother to phone the hospital for an evaluation.

The degrading interview with the psychiatrist was next. Rather than believe she was not using drugs, he labeled her distress "an extraordinarily turbulent adolescence" and did not rule out drug dependency. This was a phrase that had cost $125 an hour to hear. She had intuited the drug addiction diagnosis being discussed in the adjacent room. The white lab coat shifting quickly to close the inner office door. That horrible, familiar feeling of not being understood. Icy veins and chilly steel slabs, the hospital's anonymous deep-freeze of scientific inquiry. Whispers detached from personalities, the stifling of her inner scream. Who could possibly understand her, never mind help her? No one knew what she was talking about.

Around eighth grade it started to stalk her. An odd feeling of detachment allowed her to see her own disappearance: the part that couldn't cry or hope, watching a trail of failed prescriptions written by recommended doctors. Sedatives, stimulants, no veiling prescription made a difference. It wasn't until some disaster would befall her that her parents would rush in to save her from the latest crisis. Then there were apologies, insights. Promises.

Her judgment. Her perception. How could she trust what so often betrayed her? Why run away from home at age seventeen, other than to prove she could not survive independently?

They couldn't see it. Their baby girl. Their firstborn. Speaking sentences at fourteen months. Precocious fill-in mother for her three younger brothers. Reading people's faces before they saw her looking. Reassigned to accelerated reading by third grade. Dostoevsky by eleven. Mispronouncing words assimilated in her reading. Best baby-sitter in the neighborhood, and by sixteen, star employee at Grant's department store. They were absolutely in love with her and saw her potential actualized rather than impaired. They knew her strengths but forgave her deficits.

They could convince her, briefly, that she was normal. Between excusable lapses in reason, she was like any other teenager. This was the myth she carried into adulthood.

Mending the Fiber

While my high school classmates, now in their early twenties, were busy building homes, establishing themselves in professions, and celebrating their children's births, I lay on my parents' couch staring through the backyard window without seeing. The shimmering, sun-lit leaves rustled in the June breeze, but I was only aware of the slightly swaying branches. Someone else's story. Someone else's world.

Shapes were bland and flat, people were two-dimensional. Sounds reverberated through a multilayered filter, muffled and distorted. Colors appeared grotesque, leaping out at me as I lay frozen in my invisible block of ice. When my mother covered me with a blanket, she only covered that ice. I could not feel. It was as if the power center in my brain had been unplugged. Physically I was alive, but only marginally. Walking through a place numb, alone, in the dark, I saw the awful futility of life. Who would want to create a family in such relentless despair? Then, the next moment, it would be amusing. This is the trick the universe played on all of us humans, to know the hopelessness of life and still have to live.

Even my laughter, my own voice, detached from the rest of me. Every sound was either turned up to a deafening level or far, far away. I couldn't make decisions. I remember holding up two pairs of socks and collapsing into tears when I couldn't decide which pair to wear.

One thing that does happen in full-blown depression: you stop running. You let it catch up to you. It wants to own you. It seduces you into giving up. Then the truth is right out there for all to see. You are *no longer okay*. Depression comes with its own package of deficiencies to be worn. Particular fibers, specific weaves.

4

Adolescent Depression and the Family

OUTSIDE VIEW

The adolescent suffering from depression has an impact on the entire family. Emotional numbing blocks the perception that the afflicted are loved or lovable. Entering depression as a teenager, the young person feels misunderstood and alienated from family members, and is often angry without provocation. Depression also decreases the capacity for empathy, causing a loss of sensitivity to others. Anger originates, as in any major illness, because of the restrictions the illness imposes. Anger is caused because young people do not know what is happening to them emotionally. This anger can spill over into family relationships.

Depressed adolescents will not feel sociable, and they will participate minimally in family activities. Their energy is seriously compromised, as is their motivation to socialize. Passive activities such as watching television, constantly listening to music, laying on the sofa or isolating themselves in their rooms are common behaviors. They compensate by overeating foods high in carbohydrates, sugar, and caffeine, which give them quick energy. These rapid bursts of energy are followed by lethargy again. Younger siblings can not understand why their brother or sister no longer has the interest or energy to play with them. A cycle of deprivation begins as family members feel increasingly unappreciated.

Depression causes the insidious destruction of self esteem. Self acceptance shifts to self depreciation. The depressed adolescent finds negative reinforcement in incidental events. The family environment operates under the chronic unhappiness and boredom of the adolescent. Other children may feel they are the cause of their sibling's unhappiness. Although the family may attempt to reassure with praise and point out special gifts and skills, the depressed adolescent finds a way to invalidate these comments. "You have to say that," the depressed adolescent may claim. "You're my mother."

Depressed adolescents may feel guilty and powerless. They are wary of their personal observations and interpretations. They know their judgment has been compromised, and are often aware of their deteriorating mental health before others notice. The depressed adolescent may panic, fearing progressive impairment. A depressed adolescent will be emotionally dependent on family longer than non-depressed siblings. A prolonged adolescence may occur while classmates and younger siblings are achieving independence.

Adolescent depression often originates with family predisposition. Research has only begun to trace the long-term effects in a family's history. In the past, depression was not recognized as a distinct and permanent illness. Depressive symptoms were described as isolated personality traits. A depressed family member might be called moody, high strung, or simply nervous. Research now shows it is likely that a depressed adolescent has at least one parent who is depressed. The drawback is that the depressed parent is preoccupied, less attentive, and lacks critical energy and patience to parent. A depressed parent models minimal coping skills and a negative self image. A depressed parent may cause a minor family problem to become a crisis due to their low tolerance for frustration. Older children may be put into adult roles they are unprepared to assume.

Often a mentally well parent compensates for parental gaps left by his or her spouse by taking charge of the family, allowing the depressed parent to remain disengaged. In this situation one adult is carrying the responsibilities while the other—the cause of the imbalance—requires a great deal of special attention. The depressed adolescent is ignored.

All families endure some emotional stress during their children's adolescent years. This inevitable stress added to the problems of depressed children makes the adolescent years a crucial time in their lives. Supportive and comforting parents who help depressed children understand the illness of depression can ease the painful transition to adulthood.

Adolescent Depression Symptoms with Family

- Feels unloved and unlovable
- Displays low self esteem
- Displays communication difficulties with parents and siblings
- Is easily frustrated

- Isolates from family members
- Declines support from family members
- Reports ongoing boredom
- Displays low interest for family activities

ADOLESCENT DEPRESSION AND THE FAMILY: BRIDGE

This family section is focused on the developing child's emotional reality. Most of these poems are about my father, who was afflicted with depression and had post-traumatic stress disorder from World War II submarine combat. We missed him before we understood why he was so emotionally unavailable to us. I wrote about him in an effort to understand and discover how I might reverse this. I learned I couldn't.

The first poem is "Saddest Man." Written from my perspective as a child, it describes the experience of the emotional absence of a traumatized loved one, especially for children. "Orphan" is another angle on Dad. He was never at peace and spent his days inside history books, probably trying to understand loss and death. He was locked inside his own depression. War and grief were his steady companions.

"Inside Out" is also about Dad. Especially during my adolescence, I remember moments when he emotionally returned to us. These moments are contrasted with the violence of the hunt, one of his favorite sports, and reminded me of the emotional violence we lost him to.

"Skin Too Thin" was written as a self-observation. The skin or the protective layer that was supposed to separate me from a dangerous world in which others appeared to thrive, was missing. I often felt translucent. My skin, which was always bleeding or weeping from eczema, looked like what I felt inside: an open wound.

The poem "Ambulance" is about a little girl whose mother dies. The girl becomes an ambulance medic as a teen, searching for and hoping to rescue her mother. She relives the trauma of the imagined moment of her mother's death regularly, although she knows her mother is dead, by trying to intervene in the brief moments between life and death for the patients she speeds to the hospital. Trauma survivors often repeat the circumstances of the trauma in which they felt powerless. The person is trying to gain control over the circumstance and so goes back to it again and again, hoping to gain mastery of the experience.

"Put Down" begins with a description of suburban childhood but quickly transforms into the story of a stranger driving in a blinding, deadly storm. I remember writing this in the school library, without understanding about whom I was writing. Later, I realized that I was represented in both the driver and the car. Like me, the young woman knows the journey is significant. The vehicle is imperfect. She knows it is important to record the experience although she does not know why.

"Dark Roads" continues my journey. I speak to my middle brother, connecting a memory of a day at the sunny, welcoming seashore with the darker roads of growing up. Did he know where I went on these roads? Was he with me in darkness as he was with me that day in the sun? Would he still love me if he knew where I had been?

The last two poems are about my father's connection to me and mine to him. "Hanging On" chronicles the many ways my father taught us all to "hang on" in life. It also identifies the self-destructiveness he displayed throughout his lifelong depression. I visualized a motorcycle trip with him, one in which we gradually became equals, using the metaphor of a ride to represent life.

"Warrior's Daughter" is a newer poem, written in 1999, following my father's death. As Dad had researched warfare, I made it my goal to research depression. In this sense, I continue to address his questions about the ravages of war on the psyche. The children of war carry our ancestors' emotional past until we, the next generation, release this torment by honoring the power that fueled the destruction. Understanding depression is one strategy. Understanding the horror of warfare is another. Dad had both. Permanent damage to the psyche from combat can be partially mended by listening without judgment and accepting the traumatized individual just as she or he is.

ADOLESCENT DEPRESSION AND THE FAMILY: INSIDE VIEW

Saddest Man

War veterans stare
with a look I know too well.
It is the look my Daddy wears.
My Daddy is the saddest man.

My Daddy doesn't like loud sounds.
He gets mad really fast
when I do something wrong.
My Daddy reads war books
all day long.
He sits in his chair while the world smashes on.

My Daddy lost some of his hearing from
Pacific Sonar.
The rest he lost
to sadness.
He stands before the
Pearl Harbor Memorial at
full attention.

Orphan

In utero I heard his crying.
My dad, the darkness,
reliving those battles.
In utero
I promised
I would always hear

that urgent,
hopeless sound.

Before I could speak or read
I read his litany of losses
in startled nightmares,
desperate demands.
In the momentary tenderness
of his hand on my head
while he smoked cigarettes
like a nervous orphan.

Inside Out

My father wore his pain inside out.
He believed the world would never guess.
I was his student,
learning the subtext of
military stances,
the particular pain attached to the rigid jaw,
the frozen eyes.

When it was good,
his rigidity unlocked like giant wings,
lifting his spirit.
My father was magnificent
when he knew he was loved.

But when I trembled,
it disgusted him.
He could not afford vulnerability
in anyone.

He watched with loathing
while my hands shook

and as I crumpled,
he hated the part of himself
that felt the crumpling.

Unable to surrender to such fragility,
he walked over my pain
and with each footprint
he took
his love away as
I sliced myself up
to win him back.

My father taught me
how to read,
but never taught me
how to hide.

Sharp as the blades
of my father's hunting knives.

Skin Too Thin

She was born with her skin
too thin,
veins too close to the surface.
Veins, purple and thin as strings
trained along her face, unprotected.

She could have been an artist
or committed suicide by twenty-one.
She could have been a writer
no one understood.
Clasping her notebook to her chest,
looking down at the floor,

or staring straight through you
with translucent eyes.

Sometimes her arms would swell
with sores and
her mother gave her cream to soothe
the burning.
Called her soft names.

But her skin was too thin,
there was nothing to be done.
In the winter her hands cracked and bled
in the cold.
Her legs turned white with pink blotches
at her skirt hem.

Her skin was too thin,
there was nothing anyone could do.
Blood would rush to her head;
her veins throbbed
conspicuously.

Spontaneous nosebleeds
betrayed her.

She could barely manage
touching anyone
fearing with that touch
they would know.

And they did.

Everyone knew
about her skin.
Her brothers with their skin
strong and thick and darker.
Her father with his skin like

a leather coat.
They knew.
And it was impossible to pretend.

She tried in every way
to disappear.

Ambulance

Her mother died when she was seven,
a blazing crash.
She was not there but wondered
if she had been,
could she have saved her?

After that,
she watched for ambulances,
hoping to reach inside,
searching to recognize
the mistake that had been made,
her mother welcoming her
with outstretched arms.

The critical care siren
signals possibility to the girl.
Emergency lights
bright as the candles
of her birthday cakes
burn through the darkness.

The speed, the siren, the blinding light,
the inverse lettering of the rescue van
and her prayer:
please let me be fast enough
this time.

While the passenger,
sedated by drug-blurred dreams,
sees only
the open sky,
the rich green of the trees,
and feels
the mercy of the road.

Put Down

It had never been a bad house to grow up in. She didn't know why she had gone crazy in that house, except that it was so common, so ordinary. Split-levels alternating with ranches in neat suburban rows. It was so ordinary, she wanted to scream and in her final years, to smash something, to drive off a cliff—anything to break the rules and claim the life she never felt was hers. She would have done anything to hear the sound of life before death.

While other girls matured, she stuck close to the side of her girlfriends when they went anywhere, always knowing less than they did. Her best friend asked her if she grew up in a shoe box. She didn't know how to answer and apologized, looking away.

But tonight, the wind was howling. A screaming storm was rolling in from the coast. She drove her blue Volkswagen up the ragged hills toward the ocean, snowflakes as big as fists battering her windshield while someone or something kept repeating, "You must put this down!" Everyone knew she had no heat in the car. If the windows fogged, she would be completely blinded. She drove with the left window open in the frigid air, her head stuck out the window, snow fists slamming into her face so fast her eyes stung with frozen tears. Put what down, she wondered, when she could spare a second to wonder. Most of her seconds were filled with white terror.

The highway seemed endless. No one else was driving. She and her Volkswagen would become ice sculptures, buried in the shifting drifts of the sand-like snow. What then? Where would courage be then? As Courage whispered, "You must put this down!"

Dark Roads

Ties spun tight and descendents call,
you were my brother,
we were small and by the sea.
The sound of our ancestors
called to us.
Their melancholy.
Brother, how can anyone know
the dark roads we have traveled,
so lost in the spaces of our hearts,
so vast,
that neither time nor
distance can break the bond
that holds us fast.

The wind is cold;
it catches the leaves.
They spin and
twirl against the sidewalk.
I see all the highways,
all the seas.
What is charted,
what is not.
I see seasons changing,
people dying
for years and years
and miles and miles.

All that exists splinters like glass.
Splinters, spinning and falling,
falling at last,
until all the work
and all the days of our lives

become one pulse
of eternal energy.

We were children again
that day.
You took your pail to the water,
filled it up,
brought it back.
We laughed. We splashed.
We did not know then
that nothing lasts.

Hanging On

When I was five, Dad,
you lifted me onto your lap
to ride your motorcycle.
You told me to hang on, tight.
We crossed the Bissell Bridge
racing through
the back roads of South Windsor,
past cornfields, tobacco netting,
through the never-ending green.
And I hung on.

I hung on and learned to lean into
the dips
as you cornered,
to feel the wind on my skin,
inhale fumes, blink back bugs,
and share the joy
of the wild, fertile summer.

At fifteen, I rode in back,
clutching your leather belt

as my life preserver
through downpours,
drenching the already humid fields,
sighting storm clouds
and rainbows
in the changing sky.

Daddy, I felt your love
when you let me love
what you did.
The freedom, the endlessness
of those summer days,
the power of mid-life confidence
when you were stronger
than anyone.

We would stop,
you would smoke,
kickstand down,
leaning against the frame of your bike.
I shared your recklessness
and I hung on.

Daddy, remember that time
you were in the hospital
after your heart attack?
How you disconnected the IV,
the oxygen,
and took the elevator with me
to the main entrance
with your smuggled cigarettes?
You told me to light the match.
Breathless, I watched
the flame flicker as the security guard
radioed an alert to Cardiac.

You held you hand over mine
to steady yourself.
I hung on. Oh, Dad.

Your defiant spirit
took root in me,
sprouting ridiculous, foolish acts.
Like you,
I raced toward freedom;
running away, returning home,
never sure where to find myself.
Risking safety,
my wildness shadowed yours.

And now you face your death.
And the part of me that mirrors you
must also face extinction.
Today, I know
there will be a limit to my years,
my strength.
The days of invincibility are over.
We're just two people, Dad,
hanging on.

Warrior's Daughter

Warrior's daughter
Painting her face.
The loss will blend
with the colors
I paint.
Warrior's daughter.
Heartache.
Chest full of missing.

Praying to see your face.
Needing so much
your hand to hold,
my fingers fold
into fists.

My warrior's heart
torn, torn.
Sorrow.
Too great.

5

Adolescent Depression and Trauma

OUTSIDE VIEW

Trauma means "wound." We also use the word to mean the psychic wound or behavioral state resulting from severe emotional stress or physical injury. This kind of trauma is the emotional residue from an experience that is, or is perceived to be, life-threatening. There is an element of horror. For adolescents, such experiences include childhood abuse (both psychological and physical); threatened death, from weapons to warfare to natural disasters to car crashes; the death of a loved one; or witnessing the abuse or death of another.

The psychic injury from the horror of such experiences may be pervasive fear, emotional numbness, unexplained rage, and survivor guilt. For example, after the death of our brother John, we three surviving siblings grappled with feelings of fear, helplessness, and for me, of "Why not me?" Trauma survivors often try to forget the experience that caused it. They don't want to think about, talk about, or meet any reminders. Some trauma survivors rarely reveal the incident, but the trauma, with all its sensory details, is nevertheless left intact and vulnerable to re-stimulation through the senses. Hearing a song, smelling army rations, tasting something reminiscent of a painful time, being touched tenderly, or seeing a configuration similar to the trauma may evoke its stimulation. Sensory cues or triggers explain unprovoked violence, helplessness, or fear of imminent death for a traumatized survivor.

The unconscious does not know the difference between years ago and today. The trauma has been recorded by the observer's eye but remains unprocessed emotionally. The emotional content of the experience is inside the original memory. When we need all our senses engaged to live for the next few seconds, we are in survival mode. The more quickly the life-threatening moments are talked about and made sense of afterward, the better. The most severe damage is done to those who are continuously re-stimulated with similar traumas for a sustained time, such as those in combat.

Adolescent Depression and Trauma Symptoms

- Demonstrates cynicism
- Displays rootlessness, alienation
- Displays increasing volatility
- Perpetrates verbal and/or physical violence
- Displays lack of trust
- Displays heightened startle response
- Displays diminished awareness of bodily discomfort: cold, hunger, fatigue
- Expects foreshortened lifespan
- Disengages from community

Trauma survivors may also display biological symptoms of depression, such as difficulty concentrating, insomnia, excessive sleeping, irritability, decreased energy, or increased dependence on others. This overlapping of symptoms makes diagnosis of trauma difficult in cases where the cause is not revealed.

The symptoms of trauma are normal reactions—even animals display the effects of psychic injury—and may last for months or years. Parents can help adolescents recover from trauma by tactful comfort and support. In the case of a biologically depressed child, this help is vital. Often a counselor outside the family or a professional therapist is the child's best resource. Just knowing that others have suffered the same injury is helpful. It is important to realize that many substance abusers are protecting themselves from trauma by using drugs and alcohol. Sexual abuse is unconscionably common for young women. Healing is possible after the survivor is able to express her experience with compassionate others.

ADOLESCENT DEPRESSION AND TRAUMA: BRIDGE

"Memorial Day 2001" was written for the Vietnam veterans in Putnam, Connecticut, who visited the traveling replica of the Memorial Wall in Washington, DC. On Memorial Day 2001, I was privileged to be on-site as a trauma counselor. Throughout the day, families visited and children ran across the lawn, laughing. In addition to the replica wall, there was a trailer that displayed memorabilia of the perished. High school students studied the accompanying text. Some took notes. It is a history exhibition, unless you were a veteran.

Those who fought in Vietnam, as with most warfare, were children and teens. Shocked and emotionally betrayed by the horror of war, seeing their best friends killed, and being ordered to kill other young people leaves permanent trauma. The veterans came to the wall after nightfall. They found the names of their dead friends and traced them in pencil. They placed flowers nearby. Vietnam veterans die earlier than their peers, commit suicide in disproportionate numbers, and are more frequently and chronically homeless. Traumatized people may have frightened expressions or limited access to deeper-feeling states such as love, joy, or grief. It is not that they lack feeling. Trauma causes a loss of access to these feelings. These young people, no longer young, continue to carry survivor guilt and the intense grief of war trauma. Today, in Iraq and other war-torn regions, a toddler calmly sitting in the dirt in the street may play beside a dead parent. Horror becomes a way of life.

"What Never Happened" is another example of trauma denial. It is about a rape at knifepoint that I experienced as an adolescent. Recalling trauma is another kind of pain. Trauma recovery includes emotionally remembering the event, not as a detached observer but as a vulnerable person. At the time, I thought I would die, but surviving, I told myself it never happened. My mind recorded the trauma and concluded that any triggering memory must be avoided. Remembering would mean feeling the emotional pain.

"The Suicide Tapes" is about my father's and my depression. The characters are on opposite ends of a stage and unable to hear each other. The daughter, who has absorbed her father's war trauma to the bone, asks unspoken questions that express his emotional absence from her life: "What happened to you? Why did you leave me?" This absence is also reflected by the father's question: "Where were you?"

"Geographic Cure # 1-12" are excerpts from autobiographical writing that documents escalating suicidal ideation in a "special" community from which I believed I was powerless to escape. I dared not trust my judgment, which had been destructive to me so often. I was looking for containment so I voluntarily put myself into prison. The use of initials represents characters who are anonymous. This writing is in this trauma chapter because the focus is about the process leading up to a suicide plan. Deepening hopelessness includes the loss of connection with others, giving away prized possessions I "didn't need anymore," and relief after making a clear plan of action. The final episodes are dissociative experiences personified by Lewis Carroll's character, Alice, in *Through the Looking Glass.*

The "Walrus and the Carpenter," a favorite childhood poem, is also a metaphor for horror. All the oysters are eaten after the walrus and the carpenter convince them to take a walk. My clinical descriptions of increasing suicidal behavior are in italics.

"Chest Wall" is about our brother's plane crash in 1991. The memory of his loss pierced through my heart to my back with knife-like pain. Because he died with our uncle flying his Piper plane, I have repeated dreams of crashing, burning planes. It is also about the breast cancer I developed two years later, at my heart. The images are intermixed and incomplete. Johnny and I shared our childhood and adolescence. In our neighborhood, the houses were newly built, the trees were young, and the lawns had just begun to mature. Such newness is contrasted with the grief of traumatic memory.

ADOLESCENT DEPRESSION AND TRAUMA: INSIDE VIEW

Memorial Day 2001
(Everyone in Vietnam was wounded)

#1.
Dilapidated boots
in a showcase.
A last letter home
may display
a breath of the story.

Nothing can convey
the pain
of a vet's face.

#2.
Aluminum wallpaper
patterned with
their names
sets up, briefly,
on the town green.
The vets come
at night
in the rain
to weep.

#3.
Volunteers,
never at ease,
guard the replica
that won't remain.
The wall

that blinks back
our reflections.

What Never Happened

A sun-filled day, like today.
I was nineteen.
Elizabeth Park, mid-August, green.
I sat cross-legged
on the bank
of the duck pond.
From his car he coaxed me,
charming as the day.
Breezy smile.

Later, beyond the porch steps
of the boarding house,
door locked,
this same man,
holding a knife to my throat,
unzipped his pants
over my body now
sprawled across
a flimsy bed.
As the bathroom faucet dripped,
my mind slipped
into that bathroom.

I could see the faucet.
The clawed feet of the bathtub.
The ceiling, the dripping,
the sharpness,
the burning,
the smile, the knife

the sunlight, the pond,
the car, my life.

Today,
feeling daggers in the breeze,
my hand still guards my throat.
This never happened.
And this is how
it never happened.

The Suicide Tapes

Daughter:
(*On one half of stage, a single spot on a dark stage*)

They say that depression is a disease. Whether by heredity or circumstance, I have lived the effects of this illness, mostly alone. That's because the nature of this disease insists that you push loved ones out of your life because they would never understand.

Father:
(*Opposite stage side, unaware of daughter's presence, also in single spot on dark stage*)

They say that depression is a disease. Whether by heredity or circumstance, I have lived the effects of this illness, mostly alone. That's because the nature of this disease insists that you push loved ones out of your life because they would never understand.

Daughter:

I was born the oldest of four, to postwar parents into a loving home in the United States, one of a multitude of baby boomers whose birth followed the devastation of World War II.

Father:

(May overlap throughout piece, but should not deter audience from hearing Daughter's story, and she must provide the same clarity for Father)

At seventeen, following the unprecedented attack by the Japanese on Pearl Harbor, I knew I had to serve. My father, a lay minister, had taught me never to avoid morally responsible choices, regardless of the immediate consequences to myself. At seventeen, I clearly thought military service was the moral choice.

Daughter:

My brothers and I had every imaginable privilege middle-class American families assume without gratitude. I always felt protected, cared for, provided for, and, yes, shielded against danger—that horrible, unspoken variable that required such elaborate crafting to avoid. I could sense that desperate edge of danger: looming, vigorous, and merely hidden.

Father:

The Depression. There was no welfare at that time, remember. There was no governmental safety net, no food stamps then. Families could and did starve. During my childhood, when the market collapsed, I remember a banker, our neighbor, jumped from his office window to his death. The market crashed and he could not make good on banking commitments. There was a lot of that.

Daughter:

By seventeen, many of my contemporaries were questioning U.S. military intervention in South Vietnam. Some believed it was a civil war and the United States had no business supporting, "peace keeping," or protecting civilians who had no use for our intrusion into their homes and culture. I guess that's what might have inspired the counterculture clothing. Maybe it was young people's attempt to say to others that they did not agree with the choices or conventions of their elders.

Father:

No one despises war more that those who fight it. I witnessed the horrendous violence my fellow human beings are capable of. I never want to allow others I love to live through what I saw in those years. I don't know why I survived a burning battleship. But some of me didn't. Part of my soul is still there, with all the dead, the bodies of those men who were my brothers-in-arms.

Daughter:

Listen. This is ridiculous. On a breezy summer day I look at the fullness of the trees and see them bare. I see blood escaping from the ground beneath me. I feel cold when it is warm outside. I am alone most of the time. It's too much effort to invest in explaining myself.

Father:

Can you imagine tender flower stems pushing through blood-rich soil, tender, white blossoms whose soft petals defy the red, swollen earth, bringing innocence where there was lifelessness? This was my dream. The only one I had left.

Daughter:

I had everything.

Father:

Why was I the one who survived when the best of us died that day? And what the hell are the young doing, not sending their full support to their fellow country-men who are risking their lives to save us from communism? Do they know what communism is? Of course not! Because so many of us died defending the United States from communism. Our blood is shed for the next generation, not our-selves. I know that now.

Daughter:

He'll never fully leave that war, I know. He will never completely return home. Sometimes I believe the best of him was lost in the catastrophic violence, and we only have a shadow left. Why would I support the violence that destroys the souls of the ones who must be violent? And I don't see hope for any changes. I see a bunch of young people who stepped out of split-level houses and department stores. I see hopelessness. I see the permanent grief on my father's face, and he is looking far away.

Father:

Let me know that my children will have a better world to live in. Let them never know violence or despair. Keep them free from the knowledge I never wanted.

Daughter:

I hear it. It sounds like funeral music. It looks like the other side of the water's reflection. I am alone in this vast, seamless emptiness.

Father:

The emptiness of life. The cruelty of time: it keeps moving while we spend our lives.

Daughter:

Am I sick, Daddy? Can you help me?

Father:

I am sick with sorrow that will never cease. It is in our genes. This sorrow. This ambivalence about life. And I can't even get out of my own way.

(Both actors move closer together, finally seeing each other.)
Daughter:

Where were you?

Father:

Where were you?

Geographic Cure #1
1976

Susan walked around the store in a kind of vague, half-dream. She was there and yet she wasn't. The Christmas merchandise had been pulled and stacked in storage boxes in the basement. Susan packed it all away herself, neatly labeling each box with the contents and sealing it until the next Christmas aisle would be set.

She thought about writing her name on some paper, crumpling it up, and sticking the paper between the ceiling beams of the cellar.

(*Feeling absent, invisible.*)

It was a silly thought, something her brothers might do at the end of summer camp. "Oh, forget it," she said to herself. Although she wanted to sign her name across the store, to claim credit for the work she had done, it seemed impossible to differentiate between what she had done and what had been done by others. Confused by this, she gave up thinking about it at last and decided to set up the January promotions.

There was an open space on the floor in pharmacy that could be used for pricing merchandise, putting signs together, or other work that needed to be done from the sales floor. A small table on wheels had been set up so that people could work right in front of the department. Susan set down the sign kit—a large, flat package sealed with tape—on the pricing table, and took out her cutter.

She took the box in one hand to steady it, and with her left hand, she slowly cut through the box: a straight line through the middle.

(*Preoccupation with razors, cutting; distorted perception of the benign.*)

The store was stripped, like any other retail store in the first weeks of January. Empty shelves waited for restocking, and what was taken down because the season was over had not yet been replaced by the things for the new season. What was the next season, anyway? Susan asked herself.

"Oh shit," she said softly, stringing the signs together mechanically.

(*Images of absence.*)

Valentine's Day, that's what it was. Hundreds and hundreds of red hearts lining up like soldiers on the shelves and the hideous glitter of "I love you" all over the store.

(*Red hearts, stabbed hearts, broken heart associations. Red is associated with blood, life, love. "Hideous glitter of I love you" associates the horror of love's power to destroy, which may superficially appear beautiful.*)

Geographic Cure #2
1977

"Susan. I want you to imagine that I am the person on the other end of the line and you are calling me to resign tonight. Let's just rehearse it, as if it were a play."

"I'll practice it but that's all," Susan said. She was very close to crying. "Hello? Mr. Z?" Susan said, in a very small voice. "This is Susan from the store. I'm calling to tell you my resignation is effective immediately. I won't be in tomorrow." Susan began to cry.

V. handed the phone to L., and L. handed the phone to Susan. "Go ahead. Call him. It will only take a minute." Susan was trembling and L. reached out to hold her hand tightly.

"It's okay. You'll do fine," she said.

(First betrayal of self.)

Susan dialed the phone. "Mr. Z.? Sorry to disturb you this late in the evening." Susan didn't know what time it was, but it seemed very late at night.

"This is Susan S.," she continued. "I'm sorry to tell you that I won't be coming in tomorrow, that my resignation is effective immediately." Susan's face contorted into a twist of pain. "I know Mr. G. is on vacation, sir."

"I'm sorry, I'm sorry," she kept saying. Only when L. took the phone out of her hand did Susan realize Mr. Z. had hung up a while ago.

(Forsaking former ties, turning over personal power. Seeking surrogate family to relieve her of decision-making. Leaving surrogate family of drugstore to do so. Fundamental survival, safety issues.)

"You see how easy that was?" L. said. Susan broke down into deep heavy sobs that seemed to fill the entire building.

"I didn't want to, I didn't want to," Susan kept repeating.

"But you did, and you were wonderful!" L. said.

"You have no idea how much it hurts!" Susan sobbed.

(First action taken to surrender identity.)

"We all have to leave things behind," L. said.

(Endures manipulation of transferring loyalty from former ties to new community.)

"I was ready to leave, but in my own time, as I had planned. I can't forgive myself!"

"Would it help if you spent the night at my place?" L. asked.

"Yes. I can't go home."

(Recognizes self-betrayal.)

Geographic Cure #3
1978

Susan was driving straight into the sunset. The freeways were fairly clear for 5:00 PM. She brought an orange with her from the cafeteria and it sat beside her, in case she was hungry on the way. She rolled the window down to catch the fresh soft air. She felt the twilight begin to edge into the daylight air and it excited her. Even the green highway signs excited her. She was free, free, and it was wonderful. She had memorized the way to the teacher and watched for the signs before she switched lanes. Traffic began to congest on the freeway. It slowed, and Susan's speedometer crept down to thirty, then twenty. She looked around at the other cars. Everyone was coming to a dead stop. "Damn!" she said to herself and fumbled with the radio.

(Seeking guidance, validation.)

She wondered if the car would be okay if she only drove it once a week. She knew she wouldn't have the time or money to take care of it anymore. Maybe S. should have taken it with him. But she was deeply grateful for it at the moment, no matter how long she could continue to run it. The four wheels were whisking her to freedom, the little boat-car she and J. shared through their marriage. Susan looked around at the traffic that was stopped and began to peel her orange. If she lost time, at least she could see the sunset, she thought. She watched the sun, as round as an orange, dropping lower. It was a pleasure to see the sun after being indoors all week long.

Traffic began to pick up. Susan finished the orange and focused on driving. After about ten minutes, traffic began to thin out as cars exited off into suburbs. Soon she was driving over vast, flat stretches of highway laid out before her like ribbons. She relaxed into her seat and breathed in the air that was slowly filling with the twilight. There would be stars at the beach, she knew. Now she would be able to see them clearly.

She had been driving for forty-five minutes when she spotted her cutoff. From here, she would follow the signs to the beach. It was easy driving through the small town, and she looked at the flat openness of the land, which continued for miles, it seemed, without asphalt obscuring its loveliness. She passed several large industrial plants, but mostly it was open ground.

She saw the shopping center where her turn was coming. She made a left and continued to drive down a smaller road. The sun was almost completely down, but she hoped she could see the last moments of it before it was too late. The smell of the salt air began to reach her. She was practically there. She wound around a few town roads and turned. His house was right there, about eight houses down, on the left. She drove into his driveway and raced across the road to the ocean.

(Displays poor judgment: risks driving to a stranger's house by herself, at night, without informing anyone of her whereabouts.)

The waves crawled in like trillions of reaching fingers, grasping the wet sand of the beach. Susan did a little leap in the air and laughed. She could hardly see at all, because it was almost completely dark. The sun was gone. She was too late. Susan was sad she had missed it. "Never fast enough, but always almost fast enough," she thought. She turned to go into the house. "What's the big deal about a lousy sunset anyway?"

(Trillions of reaching fingers unable to hold on to the shore evokes inevitable loss of control.)

Geographic Cure #4
1978

And besides being so hard, it was meaningless. In Susan's mind, nothing of value could last. There was no permanence or stability to anything. So the friend she cherished a few months ago was now gone from her life, exactly as she had expected. Everything snaps, breaks, splinters off, disconnects.

(Despairing, hopeless thoughts.)

She was on the roof, and she liked it a lot better than being on the ground. She felt more at home between the earth and sky, almost floating like dust, a nobody, a nothing, an invisible spirit seeking to land somewhere. Maybe there was a shortcut off the edges of the earth from this point. Maybe someone knew the way there. She could only ask without asking, through her presence, and wait until someone heard the question.

(Assesses viability of potential site for suicide.)

Geographic Cure #5
1978

She was looking away, looking toward the roof. "This is what you had to tell me last night?"

"Yeah. You know they told me yesterday. I didn't want to tell you. But this is the way it is."

"Can I be with you today?"

"I'm leaving in a few hours. I'm sorry."

"Why don't you just get out right now then? Leave right now! What difference does it make? One hour, two hours? They're taking everything away from me! Now I don't even have you, my only friend—it's sickening! Get out of here!

Go! I don't want to look at you anymore. I don't want to remember you. Get out of here. You don't work here anymore anyway."

"Susan, I didn't ask to leave." He was turning around, leaving already.

"What am I going to do?" she said, and sat on the floor, because she could no longer stand there, looking at him.

"You'll do what you have to do."

(Emotionally triggered by perceived abandonment.)

Geographic Cure #6
1978

"You look different," he said. "Something about you."

"R. cut my hair yesterday. She shaped it."

"Not that, something else."

"Like what?"

"Your eyes."

"What's wrong with them?"

(Dead eyes, personality submerged.)

"I don't know. Never mind—ignore me. I'm glad to see you. I heard you called me last night. I was having a hard time with everything. It seemed like you were with me for an instant last night. I felt afraid for you and I couldn't sleep. You had a birthday, didn't you, a few weeks ago?"

"I guess I did. How old am I now? Twenty-three? No, twenty-four. I keep forgetting!"

"Susan, I'm terrified for you. You don't look well."

(Noticeable changes in appearance and personality.)

Geographic Cure #7
1978

The rain poured mercifully on her body. She soaked it up, watching the water pour off her fingers. She comforted herself, saying that the hardships would be over. Then suddenly it hit her, like a lightning bolt. The fact was, it was never going to get any easier here. It would always be this way. Endless, forever. She gasped, as the horrible realization slowly snuck into her consciousness. It would never, never end now. Never-ending, world without end, amen. And at that moment her face shattered into a million splinters of pain with the comprehension.

(Hopelessness.)

It was a comprehension without voice and she crumbled to the ground, gagging for breath. She would have to die. It was the only thing she had control of anymore.

(Conscious recognition of suicidal intention.)

Geographic Cure #8
1978

Susan looked at the photographs. At first she did not recognize herself and checked the small mirror at the front of the booth to see if the clothing matched. Then, as she looked again, she saw that it must be her, or a version of her in some altered state, because the features were still her own. It was like looking at an inverted negative, where all the light spots were where the dark spots should have been.

(Disassociation from body.)

At first, she was horrified because there was something hideous within the pictures. But gradually, as she continued to look at the pictures, she recognized the unmistakable look of a person who desired death. Her cheeks had sunken into her face and her eyes seemed frozen in a straight-ahead stare. Her mouth was like a line, without the muscles left to form a smile. He was right when he said her eyes were different. There was a certain savoring of this new energy of death, which held for her a peculiar delight and pleasure. She liked that her eyes were hard as rocks on her face, and thought that the supreme cruelty that the world had inflicted on her would finally be avenged in the act of self-destruction. She would have the final laugh on a universe that had rocketed her into unendurable pain.

(Distorted thinking: suicide equals revenge for life's emotional pain.)

For the past several months, Susan had missed her period. She had not realized this fact until now, however, assuming that it was a temporary imbalance that would be corrected on its own. But now it seemed only logical because she now knew her body was shutting down all unnecessary functions to sustain her for as long as possible. It made sense, for she no longer had any use for a womb. She would never give birth to new life, having lost the ability to maintain her own.

(Automatic central nervous system compromised.)

Clumps of hair bunched together as she tried to comb through it. She looked in the mirror at the top of her head and saw that her hair was thinning at the top. She never threw so much hair away in all her life. It seemed to be shedding from her, like it does with a person who has cancer. All those big globs, heaping into a wastebasket in the bathroom. "It would grow again," Susan thought. "Or it might not." It really didn't matter anymore.

(Detaching from future outcomes, expecting death.)

Geographic Cure #9
1978

She would throw herself from the roof, that was all. It would be an easy thing to do. She would sneak in when they were eating lunch. She would pretend to be using the Xerox machine and wait until they left. From the highest point in the building, it would be an easy drop, falling to the street below, but she would probably be mashed by on-coming cars. A little sloppy yet simple to do. She would be sure to die from a point in the building that high.

(Specific plan of action decided.)

Susan fantasized her death at every spare moment. She imagined what color blood she would have and if her face would finally be destroyed beyond recognition. She talked to herself in low tones as she was passing through the upstairs cafeteria where they had once served meals.

(Obsessed with her death.)

Outside the sky was tinted red, the building became submerged in red, laser-like light. The sea crept to the edges of the building, flooding the land around with a thick purplish liquid that seeped into the pores of the building, oozing, dripping down crevices, trickling into the ground-floor level, and descending lower to the deepest levels.

(Complete disassociation.)

Geographic Cure #10
1978

Winding without doors, without rooms, only walls that curved into a slope, creating a circular wall without a ceiling around and around. Was this where the dead bodies were wheeled when they failed to save them? Lining the stretchers in a neat row, placing them between heaven and hell, neither with the dead nor with the living, merely in limbo within the tunnel that stretched like a void, a chasm, a gulf of emptiness between continents.

(Psychotic state; sustained break with reality.)

The red light of the atmosphere outside glowed through the barred windows of the room, hazing over any exterior view. Through the photograph of the leader, as if looking at a negative of the photograph, she could see the form of a black crucifix holding the face and body of Jesus. The image was embedded upon the crucifix, burned into its surface as if by an iron brand. She stared into the image, tilting her head to listen. As she focused, she began to hear words from the noise that had only seemed to be a hum. The words began to come to her in shapes and sizes, in high and low tones, men and women and children, some more articulate than others, some more easily detectable, others jumbled, faltering.

(Visual and auditory hallucinations.)

Geographic Cure #11
1978

Susan drifted in a dream between day and night. She was drifting, drifting through tunnels of time between lines. She was looking for a boat to sail away in.

"Susan," the person said. Across the room the voice echoed as if spoken through a megaphone. She could not answer or even focus. She could merely stand as she was, frozen within the space. "What are you doing here?" The echoes bounced off her eardrum.

"Sit down," the voice said, eliciting no response. She felt a hand on her shoulder, guiding her down. It was a man, some man she thought she might have known at one time.

"Would your parents take you back?" he said to her. He was kneeling in front of her, searching her blank eyes for expression.

She sat where she had been placed in the chair and he reached for her hand. Her hands must have been swollen or paralyzed, because she could not feel the touch, although she knew someone was touching her.

(Distorted sensory functioning.)

"Susan! Would your parents take you back?" he shouted into her face. The sound penetrated her bones; her hand fell limply as he released it.

"Susan, speak to me. This is me, honey." The walls seemed to be contracting. Soon she would be squashed entirely. Again she opened her mouth but some tremendous force prevented her, something within her chest, her ribs, that smothered the muscles of her body.

"I, I, I, I, I've got to, I've got to, got to got to..." the sounds came from her, emerging from a guttural place, unearthly, strangling, impossible to follow.

(Disorientation of time, location, identity, recognition of others.)

"Go on, tell me. What is it?" the voice said.

Her arm lifted weakly. She held it to her throat. "I've got to, got to go back. I've got to go, go back..." she said. She reached out to touch his form; her hand seemed to be stretching endlessly before it reached him.

"To the, to the roof," she said, struggling to remember how to say words using the language she once knew so well. Her mind saw forms and shadows only, and she tried to see the words spelled out in front of her as she sounded them.

(Loss of verbal access.)

Geographic Cure #12
1978

The city had an airport colored a deep blue, reflecting like glass, connecting earth to sky, transporting people of the earth through time and space to different lands, different fields, houses and highways. Susan walked, one foot in front of the other, not sure whether she was alive or dead.

(Automatic reflexes operating.)

"I won't look back," she repeated numbly, for she felt she must be missing something, something that she should have done or known, something that was happening now, at this moment, but she couldn't feel it. She could feel nothing at all. And so she continued to be guided by him into the airplane, wondering what it was she had forgotten.

(Loss of emotional access.)

In a painless place was where she longed to be. She sat for hours, looking out the window, until at last the plane began to descend.

"What do I do now?" she asked the stewardess who passed by.

"Why, you get off here when we land," she answered.

"Thank you," Susan said to her.

They landed. She filed out, following the crowd as they stepped off the plane. As it became her turn to step out of the plane, she was suddenly surrounded by three tall men. They were her own brothers.

(Delayed recognition and response to intervention.)

Chest Wall

On the chest wall.
And the planes
were landing near the house
almost touching down.
Then the flames,
the crash.
A thousand times in dreams.

Lump removed
another year of
another cycle of
another dose of
another flight with.

He told me
to lay on my back
to look at the sky
to allow the earth
to cradle me.

But again I reminded him:
I saw the crash,
I saw the ruin,
I saw the lump,
I saw the aftermath.

6

Adolescent Depression and Addiction

OUTSIDE VIEW

Addiction is a likely scenario for the young person struggling with depression. Depression occurs when the brain doesn't produce enough dopamine, a naturally occurring manufacturer of the feelings of well-being and satisfaction. Achieving a long-term goal or completing physical exercise like jogging and swimming are examples of instances when the brain registers well-being and produces dopamine. Addicts often have less dopamine than others. Addictive drugs temporarily stimulate an overproduction of dopamine that creates a drug-induced euphoria. However, as the drug wears off, the user has even less dopamine available than before the drug use and crashes. The dopamine in the pleasure center of the brain is depleted from the drug-induced high and can cause excessive sleeping, extreme hunger, irritability, and guilt.

The use of cocaine is a perfect example of over stimulation of the brain's pleasure center. Cocaine provides a sense of invincibility and fearlessness. It can cause adolescents to remain sleepless for days. Cocaine takes away hunger and provides the missing energy a depressed young person craves. Because it also requires contact with dealers and fellow addicts, the adolescent may soon find himself in the company of untrustworthy individuals with weapons. Drug dealing is never safe. Adolescents find themselves in dangerous neighborhoods, perhaps without knowing the extent of the danger. Where there is drug dealing, there are guns and violence.

In addiction, the substance is valued over personal relationships. Money is a necessity for an addict to support the habit and dealing is the easiest way to make money. A depressed adolescent may find relief from depression and a sense of belonging by identifying themselves as a user, even though the drug-using friends are likely to be more invested in the drug than in the friendship.

Heroin, like alcohol, is a depressant that slows the metabolism by sedation. Enough of it will kill. Street drugs are never of consistent purity, and each person has a different threshold of tolerance, depending on the length of addiction, physical health, body size, and age. No one knows how much will cause an adolescent overdose. Mixing heroin and alcohol can be deadly. They are both sedatives and combining them may fatally sedate an individual.

Hallucinogens—such as LSD, PCP, Ecstasy, and cannabis—alter reality by producing visions that seem absolutely real to the user. Throughout high school, we all knew someone who had had a terrible "trip" and would intermittently have traumatic flashbacks. Hallucinogens interact with moods. If a user is frightened, angry, or despairing, hallucinogens can convert such moods into visual images. Cannabis can be either a stimulant or a depressant, depending on the user's state of mind.

In the late 1960s and early 1970s, many young people used drugs as the doorway to mind expansion. Drugs were part of counterculture behavior. What seemed like mind expansion is in reality dangerous and destructive. Drug abuse causes emotional and psychological pain. Depressed youth use drugs to escape depression. Depressed adolescents are said to be "self-medicating," but adolescent addiction can lead to wasted potential, loss of self-esteem, and foreshortened futures.

Adolescent Depression and Addiction

- Displays deterioration of personal grooming
- Demonstrates unwillingness to be specific about plans
- Angers easily
- Expresses self hatred
- Keeps company with questionable individuals
- Demonstrates unwillingness to communicate reasonably
- Uses drugs and/or alcohol to escape conflict

ADOLESCENT DEPRESSION AND ADDICTION: BRIDGE

This chapter is autobiographical, and it also contains my observations as a clinician. In my capacity as a specialist in drug addiction, I have seen overdoses, suicides, and irreversible brain and physical damage. Many teenagers who are perceived as delinquent are actually depressed and become untreated drug addicts.

The first piece, "From a Hospital Bed," is the comment of a patient on his sick bed who, due to a severe accident, was prescribed extraordinary doses of morphine, an opiate like heroin. Heroin is the preferred street drug for those who wish to feel nothing. This feeling is accomplished by blunting the open nerve signals to the brain. Because the connection of perceived pain is no longer important, there is a high risk of making decisions and following through on actions that might never have been completed without the drug. Morphine is highly addictive, and the body shifts within days from use to dependence.

"Relapse" was written about adolescents in recovery whose relapses are triggered by boredom. The life of a substance abuser is in constant danger. This can become an addiction itself in terms of heightened risk-taking, pleasure, and glamour. In this poem, the dazzle of her old addiction calls her from her home to the danger of the city where she used to buy drugs.

My next poem, "Love Was Her Drug," compares needing another person so desperately that it is a type of intoxication. The key word here is *need*. This is different from the interconnectedness of partners in which the balance of power shifts and adapts to specific circumstances. The feeling is compared to a drug fix because there is a dependence on the approval of the other to provide the altered mood. This sort of relationship is an active addiction (to a person) and is often called *codependence* in the twelve-step programs.

"Addiction" is about feeling trapped, with no sense of self, due to substance dependency. The image of being glassed in, a worthless coin rolling in dirt, expresses the degree of self-loathing of the adolescent addict suffering from depression. Addiction seeks to own a person. Addiction is a liar. Addiction seduces the user toward death.

"Lovely Lady" is about a young mother of two who spent her brief life battling drug addiction. I knew her in earlier days and was heartsick seeing her wasted face and skeletal body at the funeral parlor. The casket lining of luxurious white satin was in stark contrast with her body.

"Remember Twenty" refers to innocence lost. It is a remembrance because innocence has been prematurely lost via depression and addiction. The poem describes the absence of fulfillment experienced in both depression and addiction. Depressed young people seem to grow up faster and have fewer illusions about life turning out well for them. So many adolescents say they used to feel confident, connected, part of the world. This poem describes lost identity.

"Shadow Self" addresses self-destructive urges. Drug use, places of violence, trusting the untrustworthy are all versions of foolish risk-taking. Especially for adolescents, self-destruction is the clearest, most rational alternative to emotional pain. Drug use heightens the probability that teens will act on suicidal ideation.

Finally, "Dialogue with Addiction" is an internal struggle between the healthy self and the destructive self, personified as a booming, disconnected voice. In addiction counseling, it is referred to as the "sober self" versus "the addict self." It is an internal struggle between the desire for emotional health and the immediate reward of feeling better that addiction provides.

ADOLESCENT DEPRESSION AND ADDICTION: INSIDE VIEW

From a Hospital Bed

"Morphine doesn't take the pain away. It's just that you don't care about it anymore."

Relapse

At the laundromat,
folding her Frampton T-shirt,
she abruptly realized
she would be folding laundry weekly
for the rest of her life.
And every week,
she would buy vegetables to steam
and curry powder for the organic food
in her clean-living diet.

And as she visualized
all the trips to Waldbaum's
and all the liquid YES! she would pour,
the repetitive monotony of her life
filled her with vacuous horror.

Later, at home,
her dripping faucet became
uncompromisingly relentless.

And when her mirrored face
stared back with the absent eyes
of her deepening trance,
the seductive voice of her old, old lover
whispered,

"Take me to Springfield.
I will dress you in party shoes
and you will glitter
with me inside of you,"
and she was powerless.

Love Was Her Drug

Love was her drug.
She was intoxicated by
the timber of his mumbling
and how
his hips moved inside
that smooth, snappy stride.
He was electric
and she was plugged in.
Love was her drug.
And she was in love.

Only love arrested pain,
like a dark-suited cop
handcuffing loneliness,
taking it prisoner,
lifting the burden of time,
easing her into that seamless space
of perfect oblivion.

Love was her drug.
Other women understood.
Other women would give it all
for those ecstatic moments of
absolute desirability which
she mainlined
with his hungry glances,

guarantying
her worthiness
for yet another moment.

Love. Love was her drug.
She could never get enough
of that sweet substance, love.

Addiction

I am enclosed in a glass case,
disembodied voices scream my name.
Addiction says I am worthless.
Am I?

I roll like a penny
down the street,
the dirt, the road
crusts over me.
I want to disintegrate.
Can I?

Each night the cars pass by
in the dark.
I stay inside,
become the house.
I want to breathe,
I want to feel
but it takes so much,
so much to heal.

Lovely Lady

Lovely lady,
sliver-thin hands

wrapped in Rosary,
blue angel dress,
a cloud above the casket lining.

Youngest son sleeping,
older son staring.
Sweet, hopeful girl
where did you go?

Wasted thin face,
jaw line jutting
unsupported bones,
orphan child
of the street,
in two hours' time
you will be gone.

Lovely lady,
I knew your beauty,
your puppyish humor,
your mother's dreams,
your search for safety.

Soon your fragile corpse
will leave the church
and be buried,
too soon.

Remember Twenty

Remember twenty
before the leaves
fell all around you,
before you knew
how to run.

Remember twenty
before the sickness.
Before the prison inside freedom,
before death
in life.

Remember twenty
when anything could be imagined
and anything imagined,
found.

Remember twenty,
before the losses,
before the fear,
escaping only one person;
yourself.

Shadow Self

Vacant midnight
searching to find you
draped between stale green curtains
again.

It was so dimly lit
I could barely see,
there, in our room,
your presence.
Repeating, twisting,
a melody from a song
I could not recall.
Somewhere in the half-light
you housed yourself in my mind

luring me in dreams,
calling me from some shadowed stairwell.

Tripping on the carpeting
rolled up in some dingy bed.
Between the boards and shelves
you disappear again.

If I hunt every
address on earth,
I may never find you,
obscured by
veils and fears
until time tricks me
and
once again
I see your reflection.

As sunlight moves
through my days,
mostly, I forget you.

Until moonlight
dances on my wall. Then
I begin to remember,
my shadow self,
why you terrified me.

And why,
as I stood,
on the edge of terror,
I loved you.

You called me crystal,
you laughed at me
when I couldn't see

in the dark.

You screamed obscenities to me,

waiting for me

to fight back.

Dialogue with Addiction

"You liar, you thief, you hypocrite, you cheat, you monster, I'm going to…"

"Shut up, get back, get back down."

"I'm going to get you when you aren't watching. I will sneak in."

"I'm fine, I'm protected, you will not get me, I will fight you."

"Listen to me. You've been bad. You've wanted what you have no right to want and that makes you bad. I'm going to fix things so you cannot sleep nights. I'm going to fix you so you'll always be afraid. That ought to fix you."

"I hate you! Get out of my life! You're destroying me. I don't want to walk around with you all the time."

"I'm bigger than you are and you know it. I told you I'm going to get you. I'm going to disable you. I want to see you overcome. Take this guilt! Here! Here! Here!"

"Get out of my universe: this room, this house, this life!"

"But you invited me."

7

Adolescent Depression and Suicide

OUTSIDE VIEW

The disease of depression, which is caused by a chemical imbalance in the brain, distorts logic, crushes self-esteem, and robs a person of energy and resilience. The deeper the depression, the more the personality is submerged. Depressed teens, believing that they will never get better, often sink into despair. Despair leads to suicidal thoughts, also called *ideation.*

Since mental illness often manifests itself in the early teen years, many depressed adolescents have no prior history of depression. Their parents may not recognize the disease of depression and are likely to see children's antisocial behavior as deliberate provocation. The children, already feeling that the painfulness of life is too much to bear, feel shame for causing the family distress. To the thought of "I can't go on living" they mentally add "they'd be better off without me." And their parents are unaware of this dire situation.

In trying to determine if an adolescent is suicidal, parents should know that adolescents do intend and attempt suicide. Some succeed. Often, they have expressed their intention, although they may have contradicted the assertion with undermining statements. They must be taken seriously when they express a wish to die. Sometimes no warning is given, so parents must be on the lookout for indicators of suicidal intention. A family history of depression or suicide is an important indicator. So are dysfunctional family situations like child abuse (especially sexual), violence, alcoholism, and a reversal of the parent-child relationship.

Adolescent Depression and Suicide

- Feels a burden to others

- Thinks there is "no way out" of emotional pain
- Abuses drugs and/or alcohol
- Believes they have experienced a major failure in school, home, or relationships
- Suffers from teasing, disrespect, or lack of support from peers
- Experiences sexual identity crisis
- Demonstrates unreasonable expectations of self or others
- Has access to weapons, poisons, or other lethal implements

A parent who identifies several of these suicidal intention cues should make intense efforts to build the child's self-esteem and seek the child's confidence. If these efforts fail, the parent should immediately get professional help for the child by bringing him or her to the emergency room. If the adolescent is an imminent danger to self or others, hospital admission is necessary. Individuals who are suicidal may become instantly homicidal. An adolescent may be unaware of suicidal ideation and still be suicidal. Do not hesitate to take action. Depression is a progressive and potentially fatal disease.

ADOLESCENT DEPRESSION AND SUICIDE: BRIDGE

The common theme in these poems is self-destructiveness. The first poem, "She Wanted to Die," was written at seventeen, following my three-month disappearance that ended with an Interpol intervention in London, where I had fled. When I wrote the poem I felt like an expatriate of humanity.

"I Hear a Voice Who Wishes Me Dead" is about internalized self-hatred and self-rejection. It is the same voice from Chapter Six's "Shadow Self." These internal critical tapes, which we all have, are particularly disabling for a depressed teenager. Depression negatively slants perspective. If the individual has had a history of being criticized and belittled, such mental tapes can be devastating. My tapes played very loudly for me throughout the darkest times of my adolescent depression.

"The Rooms I Could Not Escape" is not only about the walls of a hotel suite in London, but the trap of my own psychic rooms. I despaired about life ever improving. Either I outrageously pursued self-damage or I was bored and disinterested in what other teenagers so enjoyed. I was cycling between high and low without knowing when I would suddenly feel manic or hopeless. Suicide became a possibility when I could not see a way out of suffering. I felt that all of the details began to mean something: the burning candle, the locker number in Heathrow airport, the writing that seemed to erupt from my soul, the belief that no one loved me or ever could. Depression was greedy. It required me to focus exclusively on it.

A depressed adolescent is focused internally, leaving little ability to empathize with others. When I went to London, I did not remotely understand what I had put my family through until I returned home and began treatment. I was surprised they had missed me.

"Blue Black Night" describes the emotional battering I experienced in depression. It documents powerlessness and concludes with being swallowed by the night. Depression, death, darkness, and black-and-blue bruises no one seemed to see.

"Death in Silence" was written following the funeral of our father. The mouth of death, represented as an open grave, speaks soundlessly.

The poem "Glass Case" uses the metaphor of entombment within self destructive urges. The contradictory impulses to stay alive and to die are equally compelling.

"Slamming" is my overview of the power of depression and my struggle to kill it. Unfortunately, it is not possible to kill an aspect, trait, or illness and remain alive.

Adolescent Depression and Suicide: Inside View

She Wanted to Die

She was a smile sifter,
a lifetime loner,
a sugar sharer,
a crippled crayon.
She was the one
who got A's in compliance,
and when she grew up,
she wanted to die.

She wanted to color inside the lines,
walk on the right side of the road,
fall in love with someone brave,
her life wrapped tightly as a braid.
But when she grew up,
she wanted to die.

She was always strong too late,
she was always fast too slow,
she was always going somewhere else.
How much courage does it take?
More than she
would ever know.
Is there a reason to stay alive
if the reason is not your own?

I Hear a Voice Who Wishes Me Dead

I hear a voice who wishes me dead.
I hear it over and over again.

It asks me to go back to the place
I began. The nothingness.

I love his voice.
I will do as he says.
I know he loves me;
he is all that I am.

His voice fires a bullet
through my heart.
This strange, single bullet
of love
is all I've ever known.

The harsh, blinding light
snaps on,
a glimmering blade.
We seek our death
in different ways.

To return to where the wind
swirls our shadows.
Back to the place
without time.

To walk through those open doors of death,
those corridors of wind
looking through nothingness,
knowing
it will never matter again.

The Rooms I Could Not Escape

I am trying to remember the room I could not escape. Dark, heavy, floral curtains, probably a century old, converted daytime to darkness. A neighboring brownstone building, looking as if it was only feet away, was effectively disguised by those curtains. One window was secured with protective iron bars. Another curtain hung in front of the bed: solid mahogany velvet, theatrically high, draped from its curtain rod by wide, imposing rings. Ornamental, baroque. It could be drawn shut for private sleep in the small, truck-stop uncomfortable bed. A parlor area with a round wooden table and two battered, throw-away stuffed chairs, the color of some horrid green, were where we sat.

A separate area for grooming. Another area with bath, toilet, and bidet. Our white candle in the center of the table. The phone, half tangled in the curtains at the base of the hem.

I was there: emotionally numb, away from home, and sleep deprived—enough to be convinced there was some special purpose for our erratic behavior. I was hypnotized by a belief in my uniqueness as we went deeper and deeper inside our shared grandiosity. I was seventeen. He was older. We believed we were psychic. I now think we were in the midst of a shared mania or psychosis that we reinforced in one another.

It was all my latest attempt to justify life. It didn't look that way to Interpol. We were sent home within a week. Sent home to face the repercussions of our poor judgment, which caused so such emotional damage to others. If only I had psychiatric medication then, maybe we would have been all spared this pain. Instead, we carried it into every room, every inescapable room, of depression's early symptoms in my life.

Blue Black Night

It was dark, a blue black night.
A girl's shadow crossed
a rusty track,
nothing was clear but
this twisting ache.
They said I would break,
I told them I wouldn't.

Because the ground
was a bottomless pit,
because all she could see
were her hands and feet,

she laughed.
It made no difference.

Lift up your arms
to the gods of despair,
fall on your knees beneath,
and when you are sure
nothing is left,
offer yourself to me.

And now it was time
to ask for a hand
when no hands were left to ask for.
And now was the time
to fight for strength,
when nothing was left
to fight for.

Oh gracious, merciful, generous god
if you are somewhere around,
it wasn't them who defeated me
but myself,
just myself, how I am.

And inside her head,
visions floated like dust
invisible to anyone's sight,
and inside her heart,
as hope disappeared,
she was swallowed
by the night.

Death in Silence

Death arrives in silence,
directing the world to stop.
And death steals my love
whenever my loved one is lost.

And death meant to pull me
into death's grave
and I trip
and I trip
over the open grave of death.

Death looks like summer
and white satin crepe.
Dark cherry wood,
a freshly dug grave.
And death orders gunshots
and Taps by the grave
and death will not add
to anyone's hours.
Death
smells like flowers.

We who yet live
on death's silky side
challenge the power of death
when we love,
when we cry.

So disturbing,
so edgy.
So sure of our stride.
While death comes
in silence.

Glass Case

Like a butterfly
paralyzed
within a paperweight,
or some impurity
within metal,
I am imprisoned
within myself,
a staircase descending,
forever.

Wanting to break through
this case of glass,
but frozen in time,
this other place threatens
to choke me alive.
But not before
it has grown teeth,
yawning
it's vast vociferous mouth.

Slamming

Slamming against those
ancient, webbed walls,
fragmented,
mirror-sharp,
razor-edge walls.

Will I always replay
this story?

The jagged landscape prods me,
I am the landscape.

I'm slamming against
insanity,
walking the inside walls
of me.

8

Adolescent Depression and Recovery

OUTSIDE VIEW

It would not be honest to say I received treatment and spontaneously improved. Depression is more like the illness of addiction—the individual remains susceptible to relapse throughout his or her life. However, teens can learn which symptoms signal a recurring depression for them and catch the progression earlier. Less flexibility with others, more time spent isolated from peers, changes in hygiene, and a shift in the adolescent's family involvement are all potential signs. A recent disappointment can be taken out of proportion and generalizations like "I'm just a failure at everything" become cognitive distortions. Some other triggers for recurring depression might be the anniversary of the death or loss of a loved one, loss of a trusted therapist or a supportive friend, relocation, discontinuing medication, or a subjective feeling of betrayal, abandonment, or abuse.

Despite these on-going challenges, depression is treatable. As I learned in my late twenties, quality of life can be profoundly improved. The combination of cognitive therapy, which addresses a depressed teen's distortions, and medication management elevated my level of functioning.

As a depressed teen, I quit college after two years. I didn't have the energy or confidence to pursue it further. Finally in treatment by my late twenties, I returned to the University of Connecticut for my undergraduate degree, went immediately to Central Connecticut Graduate School, became a graduate student teacher, and began teaching in a community college by the time I was thirty. I was able to return to theater as a director and spent the next decade teaching and directing. I am willing to wager that without treatment I would have remained in retail, which is physically more demanding and mentally less challenging. In my forties, I certainly would not have sought a second master's degree if I had not experienced success as a college teacher. By this time, I considered myself functioning to my potential. I was eager to find new areas of study that would continue to challenge me. After receiving my master's in counseling from Saint Joseph College, I was immediately hired by the agency where I had interned.

Had anyone told me at twenty that I would become a teacher and a leader, I would not have believed her. Had anyone told me my teenage writings would become the springboard for communicating my struggle with depression to other young people, I would not have believed him, either. Actually, I wouldn't have believed anything positive about myself. The gradual and difficult work of examining assumptions and trading them for affirmations took me a long time. Like many others who are prescribed antidepressants, I took myself off my meds, always crashing within two to three months. It took me a while to comprehend that this was a diagnosis from which I would never be "free."

This information has allowed me a lead a rewarding life. Because metabolism slows down in depression, life energy is depleted. Alternative behaviors and "escape plans" are vital. Have a support system of friends and older adults to confide in. Be especially careful of far-fetched schemes or getting better instantly. Remember, depression compromises judgment, and your viewpoint will be slanted pessimistically. Depression tells you things will never get better. This is a symptom of the disease!

Know yourself and trust your instincts. If sex is likely, know what your answer will be and protect yourself accordingly. Sex does not cure depression and may deepen it if you feel manipulated or deserted by your partner. Don't go to that dance if you feel uncomfortable. Listen to your inner voice—the voice that says you know you can reach your potential.

Be persistent in the search for help. There are some medical professionals who do not recognize depression in an adolescent. The shortage of adolescent treatment centers attests to the lack of attention paid to these developmentally critical years. But help is available. If nothing exists in your community, consider forming a "transition" support group with peers. In this group, members agree to provide feedback to one another, especially when someone appears to be in jeopardy. It is easier to see depression in one another than in yourself.

Depression may creep up gradually without "feeling" like depression. It may feel as if you just can't try anymore. Adolescents have the fewest resources to cope with depression yet are expected to outgrow symptoms without treatment. Untreated depression continues to cause damage to self and others due to poor judgment, risky behavior, and a lack of concentration and focus. It can developmentally delay adulthood, as it did in my case. Depression views life as a permanently intolerable condition. It is unrealistic to expect self-advocacy from a person who can barely tolerate getting out of bed. That is why it is so important to be able to reach out for help. If you are feeling unsafe, go to the nearest emergency room. There is psychiatric help in any U.S. hospital, but it is important that your symptoms not be trivialized. Shifts in brain chemistry distort perception and judgment. The attendant emotional numbness leads to difficulty and a tendency to misinterpret another's motives, as well as a lack of awareness that anyone cares. Life affirms love, joy, growth, and abundance. Depression reinforces despair; a distracted, "not present" existence; a focus on past losses; regret, or fear of impending sorrow. Depression polarizes the individual to cease caring for himself by minimizing or discounting positive comments made by others. Selective hearing and distorted self-image negate reassurance.

For these reasons, therapeutic treatment must be nonjudgmental, supportive, and empowering. The therapist temporarily provides this healthy interior voice that insists on the inherent worth of the person, despite emotionally maintained distortions. The depressed individual may insistently express the desire for isolation. Yet, there is an accompanying awareness that self-regulation is gone and there is a need for regulation by others.

Adolescent variables include the young person's knowledge of the depth and range of the depression. The fear in parents and caretakers may exacerbate depressive symptoms, making it more difficult for the depressed young person, who will not have the resilience of her peers. Adolescent depression can be misdiagnosed as drug abuse, drug addiction, antisocial behavior, attention deficit disorder, lack of respect for authority, willful disrespect, lack of attention at school or at home, or it can be minimized as a "developmental phase."

The past few decades have provided the prescriptive ability to regulate and control the brain dysfunction of depression via antidepressants. These drugs help modify the brain's underproduction of mood-regulating chemicals. A depressed individual will not become intoxicated on such a drug, as many parents fear. An antidepressant will not cause drug dependence. Depressed individuals often find that the antidepressants are needed for insight-oriented therapy, which examines negative thinking and how distortions affect life choices, identity, and relationships.

The disease of depression is treatable. However, it is not always easy to recognize. The following material will assist with the compassionate identification, expression, and treatment of this disease in young adults.

Healthy Adolescent Mental and Emotional Traits

- Demonstrates flexibility
- Displays realistic expectations of self and others
- Values life and lives of loved ones
- Is emotionally available
- Maintains self-esteem, neither grandiose nor self-deprecating
- Displays stable sense of self regardless of changing circumstances
- Experiences a range of emotions (sadness, disappointment, anger, joy, gratitude) and is free to express a wide range of feelings
- Accepts emotional boundaries of self and others while maintaining appropriate social boundaries
- Employs humor to deal with difficult situations
- Demonstrates personal resiliency

ADOLESCENT DEPRESSION AND RECOVERY: BRIDGE

It is difficult to describe "unthawing" from depression. Depression teaches adolescents to face mortality sooner than their peers. It is a mood-altering state like chemical dependency, but it is not the same and requires different treatment. I have collected this material with the hope that adolescents will find comfort reading about things they may feel and my journey in overcoming them, written in a loving, first-person voice that could be their own. I believe depression comes with a wonderful bonus. Adolescents who are depressed are often more self-aware, more apt to be artists, more likely to create from tragedy. Depressed adolescents can have an immense capacity for empathy and a gratitude for life, a quality that some peers might not develop in youth.

This material has also been collected for parents of the depressed adolescent. It is in the interest of your child and your mutually continuing relationship that depression is identified as depression and that you seek treatment. There are many ways an adolescent may display depression. The severity of these traits will indicate how out of control the adolescent feels. Help is available. Partial lists of resources and suggested reading are presented at the end of this book.

The final chapter is about discovering wellness. This writing flows into the present. The first two poems, "Autumn" and "Random Fortune," are about accepting loss as part of the sacred journey of life. Depression asks its recipient what is important enough to live for. Depressed adolescents face this question early in their lives and must answer it out of necessity.

"Love Song to the Night" was written twenty-five years ago, when I could not imagine being fifty years old. It seemed to be coming out of nowhere, so I held on to it. Now, at fifty-one, it reflects my motivation to "carry the love song into the night." The woman was my future self.

"The Changing Room" is specifically about radiation treatment. I was diagnosed with breast cancer at forty-one and was once again looking at mortality. It had become clear to me by then that my spiritual journey was about honesty, loving, and letting go. Confronting cancer, I was able to discover what work was most important to me. Knowledge of the impermanence of life has been a great incentive for me. "Landscapes" is a soul flight with my brother, John, whose death taught me the transcendence of the spirit.

"Birth" is about spiritual rebirth and transformation. It is waking up in the morning, knowing you are lovable, loving, and loved. Next is "Laconia." After a special day with my brother, Billy, and our dad at the Laconia, New Hampshire motorcycle races, I wrote to John, who loved Laconia and had accompanied Dad. Laconia motorcycle racing takes place annually on Father's Day. The poem is about our family's love for each other, and the invitation to include memories of John to walk with us that day. "Amanda" is about John's daughter. At the time, she was nine. Now in high school, it is wonderful to see her on-going resiliency and passion for life.

"Love" is about looking into a beloved's eyes and seeing warmth. I have been richly blessed by love. Love explains my own survival and, later, my joy. "Four Women," written in 1982, is a vision of maturing stages progressively melting together. The first woman is ripped open. She is vulnerable and raw. The second calls for help but is not heard. The third begins to find feelings of anger surface beneath her depression. She challenges depression to a battle. The fourth woman is able to look outside herself and see the beauty of life surrounding her. "Woman in Rain" is a joyful image of triumph, written after I started treatment. I envisioned a beautifully swirling dancer, spinning in the rain, everything in motion, feet on the ground, laughing.

ADOLESCENT DEPRESSION AND RECOVERY: INSIDE VIEW

Autumn

Between maturity and decline,
autumn comes.
Autumn comes on the fragrance
of clear, dry air
and in this astounding moment before we leave,
a rainbow of regrets
bursts through complacency
glistening defiant colors:
reds, oranges, yellows.

And if we are empty enough to feel them,
our losses reappear.
In autumn we are asked to awaken.
This time, knowing permanence is a lie.
Knowing clearly winter
will be here,
what it feels like,
how unprepared we are.
And how, most of all,
the early beauty that was here
is gone.

And we are left with autumn.
Before the freezing of the ground.
When the bravest flowers
stand alone. Sacrificial.
Count blessings
with open eyes.
In preparation.

Limitation.
Gratitude.

Random Fortune

Welcome the balance
of life and death,
honor the two-faced deity.

See the three generations
shifting places with the next
until it is each one's turn
to journey to death.

Who,
having accomplished survival
into old age
through random fortune,

having probably awaited
for the spectacular
to occur,

discover the deeper,
more compelling need
for rest,
and the world
less urgent.

Love Song to the Night

From death to life
the memory etched on her face
forever present
in waking and in sleep,

she traveled with the memory of death
tugging at her sleeve.

She escaped through a chasm,
a hole in the prism,
sped through corridors
transported by light.

She was crystal,
transparent as film,
weightless within
a water drop.
The color of love is light.
The body of love is light.
No one may measure
the power of love.

Go back, they said.
Go back to the world,
you must go back.

There were cracks in the earth;
erosion
split the ground.
The air was dirty,
smothered in sound.

She could barely hear
the moon bird cry.
We are in danger.
We are in fear.
We are in terror.

The air was trembling.
The light was trembling.
The space within space

pulled her back
like a vacuum,
crushing bones,
constricting skin.

She was born a woman
in a hospital bed
her body was fifty years old
her eyes gently opened.

The light within her
fought disease.
Healing, mending,
making whole
those who were broken,
that which was cold.

She carried the love song
into the night.
She carried the love song
into the night.

The Changing Room

The doors swing shut as I
enter a suspended universe,
a radiation holodeck
where,
shedding my street clothes
in the changing room,
I am
an anonymous gown.
I seat myself beside
other gowns,

reading *Prevention* magazine.
Waiting.

It is no time of day
in this place
and no one has an age.
A white-haired, thin woman
tells me she's "pissed off"
with her husband
for not allowing her to drive.
I comfort her like a doting aunt.

A young woman removes her cap.
Her head, bald as a newborn's.

The gowns, the blue marks
on our chests, throats,
private places
bind us
in this abrupt fellowship
in which
shy people speak frankly,
independent people learn limits,
aggressive people
become gentle,
vocal people become quiet.

Which is why
we smile across at one another
in the vacant placelessness
of the changing room.
We are in a place
that is no place.

Street noises, daylight,
or at nightfall,

people busy with *agendas*
remain outside this door.
While we anonymous gowns
wear the finiteness
of our lives.
And grow compassion.

Landscapes

The dreams are landscapes
connected by threads of light.
The landscapes are dreams
connected by threads of light.

There is no landscape to own.
Not the rivers
not the houses
not the roads.

Sacred spirit in me,
who flies beside her brother,
joyously laughing
as green fields fade,
knows.

Endless blue of the day-lit sky
lift me
from self-importance
into your generous arms.
Let me lose
significance
in your magnificence.

Birth

By the edge of the river
there is a birth.
There is a birth by
the edge of the water.

A fragile egg
in my hands
is born into light
by the edge of the water.

By the edge of the river
there is a birth.
There is a birth by
the edge of the water.
And no one
seems to know
but me.

And no one hears
my unformed words.
And I am a dreamer
floating in time,
drifting and dreaming,
shifting in time.

I cry to the wind
but the wind cannot hear me
I open a door
yet no one can see me.
Somehow, this birth,
so staggeringly real,
is real to no one but me.

That day I discovered
what was to be born.
To feel life in my hands.
To hold grace
and strength
that is not meant
to be kept.

I have cried and cried in pain
for the sorrow this life brings
for wanting and needing
for keeping and holding
that which is not born
to be kept or held.

Can anything live
without changing?
I am born.
Another part dies.

Laconia
In memory of John

Once a year
the New Hampshire International Speedway parking lot
roars and spills
a sea of bikers to the fences.
In that ocean
Daddy, Billy, and I bob
without you.
Today, Daddy has a portable oxygen tank
I position on his shoulders.
Billy injects doses of insulin for him.
BUT

Billy mimics the British announcer
who favors the *doo-kaaa-deee*
so much he misses the other twenty racers.
And we howl!

We bake
on shadeless bleachers
like white bones in sun
but today Daddy is no longer seventy and failing.
He hikes the length of the track
to watch the tightest cornering.

"The bravest men in the world,"
he laughs.

Caught up in the joy
I threaten to show my tits on demand
to roadside spectators.
To my delight, Billy feigns shock,
insisting "only the men comply."
Oh John, you should have been there.

Harley Davidson has a new
competitive racing one thousand
(they haven't got the glitches out yet)
the Ducatis, Suzukis, and Kawasakis
were faster.

The one thousands blew by the fence at 140 mph.
With each lap we imagined ourselves
in full leathers.

Daddy says the six hundreds ran like toys.
Billy ranked the one thousands.

John, John,
you would have loved it.

Amanda

Amanda girl, age nine,
who orders a Grand Slam for breakfast,
"the usual,"
who flips like a rubber band
on her trampoline,
who thoughtfully suggests
Uncle Clark might like
that Mickey Mouse tie,
whose albino rabbit, Snowflake,
adores her.
Amanda, who reminds
Aunt Kathy she's
"stuck in the seventies,"
who wears Nancy Sinatra boots
to be filmed,
who snuggles like a snuggle bun
in unexpected moments,
who describes her dress as "pleasant,"
who eats frozen peas
from a cup,
who would like a Beanie Baby
from Canada,
even though she lives in
the United Steaks of America,
who found a forty-dollar lizard
in a toy shop,
who knows she could make a lot
of money selling
Fort Devens trucks
for a thousand dollars each,
who throws all her irrepressible

energy into
each original today,
whose hand waves from
the back-seat window
from Mirror Lake
to Route 111,
I love you.

Love

A childhood breeze
renewing trust
a rush of heat
from inside out
stabs the chest
realizing you are known.
And being known,
you are forgiven.

Within the imperfect hours of now
the miracle exists;
you will always need allowances
and there is someone
who cares enough
to make them for you.

A bath of light.
Perfect breath.
The ordinary shimmers
with color and energy;
comfort within
danger.
Ordinary. Familiar.
Oh, yes. There. There it is.

Four Women

Woman One:

I need you so much. I need to feel your arms around me. I need you to surround me. I need to be consumed with you. I need to know you'll be consumed by me. Make me whole. Make me love. Make me see.

Woman Two:

I am empty. I am lonely. I am a doll without stuffing. I am a wound knocked open. I am the dust that is floating. I am nothing filled with nothing. I am worthless, helpless, hopeless. I am soft flesh mashed by stone.

Woman Three:

I am big and strong and real. I am angry; I am here. I remember bleeding, crying, crawling, screaming. I have this right to remember! I have this right to feel. I am a feeling, grown-up woman. I am here.

Woman Four:

I see the buds that open. I see arms unfolding. I see tones and shades expanding. I see circles, blending, growing. I see light and shadow forming. I have peace inside for caring. Relentless time, be kind. Let me complete the work that is mine.

Woman in Rain

The feet that stopped running,
rushing to death prematurely,
stand still and press
firmly into the warm earth.

The woman allows the rain
to fall softly on her,
soaking up moisture,
the clean, fresh raindrops.
And then,

breathing deeply,
hearing the music
of the rain,
she begins to dance.

She plays herself.

Drops of water
drip from curls
and clothing.
Mud splats.

She lifts her arms
she swoops and spins,
permitting herself,
propelling herself.
She weaves, she reaches,
she gathers,
dancing
circles in the rain,
the mud,
the earth.

Dancing because she is
a woman in rain.

9

Adolescent Depression

CONCLUSION

Thirty-seven years ago, it was unlikely for an adolescent to be diagnosed with depression. Instead, he or she was labeled "conduct disordered," "troubled," or even "psychotic." In my adolescent years, such assumptions by parents, teachers, and health professionals further ruptured my fragile self-esteem.

Today, many improvements have been made in the treatment of adolescent depression. There are agencies that specialize in teen treatment; some even include their own academic services. You may find an inpatient adolescent unit within a larger hospital psychiatric department. There are after-school programs in which the adolescent remains in school but is transported to the supportive programming of group counseling, individual counseling, on-going psychiatric monitoring, and medication management. Often, such treatment is reimbursable. If insurance is not available to the patient or family, there are free clinics. If you are ever turned down for insurance reasons, ask for other sites that will accept your coverage. Money should never be a reason to go untreated.

Immediate treatment is required if there is imminent danger, *i.e.* suicidal ideation or behaviors that display intention of harm to self or others. They need an emergency room where they can report their symptoms as specifically and completely as possible. There will be a psychiatrist on duty and a process by which that hospital can refer and transfer them to an appropriate site.

To recap, look for these indicators.

Adolescent Depression Symptoms

- Decrease in peer interaction
- Demonstrates over-reaction to every day events
- Displays declining concern for good eating habits

- Experiences greater interpersonal conflict at home and with peers
- Displays preoccupation with past or future failure
- Is promiscuous
- Practices risky behaviors, including alcohol and/or drug consumption
- Expresses preoccupation with death

Professional caregivers for adolescents ought to be aware of and on the alert for such symptoms of depression, so they are able to distinguish an irritable outburst or passing intolerance from deepening depression. Family histories of depression, gathered as part of the teen's medical profile, can inform professionals when self-report is difficult. As a depression progresses, the person's functioning regresses. Expecting the adolescent to come forward, take medical action, tolerate the frustration of rejection from one site and then pursue another may be asking too much. A teacher, counselor, or parent can help facilitate an appropriate placement. Observe, ask questions, and compare behaviors with those of other teens. The inability to follow through could be a symptom of depression. Skill building to be able to tolerate frustration, problem solving, and positive affirmations are all part of effective treatment. These skills can be learned. A rampant adolescent depression needs intervention. Intervention and treatment are available.

Glossary

Adolescent: A developing young person from age thirteen to nineteen, often extending emotionally through the mid-twenties. This stage of maturity is crucial for establishing self-identity and consequently, adult functioning. Higher-level, abstract thought is maturing.

Battered child/partner: Any individual suffering from verbal, sexual, or physical abuse at the hands of a trusted loved one. Consequences include broken bones and permanent neurological and mental damage, and can lead to death.

Bias: Preexisting attitude or assumption toward a particular topic.

Clinical: Material and applied knowledge in a specific area of expertise. Usually requires a specific degree, certificate, or internship.

Denial: An inability to perceive certain circumstances, factors, and/or fears in an effort to avoid admitting their existence. It involves overlooking obvious circumstances that others observe so that the behavior or belief may continue.

Diagnosis: Physician-determined physical and mental health status, including both physical and mental disorders.

Experiential: First-hand experience recreated to directly access the sensory (audio, sight, smell, taste, touch) components for the participant.

Imminent danger: Immediate life-threatening circumstances for self or others.

Indicators: Specific symptoms that support a particular diagnosis.

Malaise: Lack of interest or energy for previously enjoyed activity. An observable, metabolic shift from a person's usual energy.

Overdose: The ingestion of a lethal combination of toxic substances.

Post-traumatic stress disorder (PTSD): See *trauma.*

Suicidal ideation: The emotional state in which the individual believes suicide is the only alternative to life problems.

Suicidal plan: The specific, premeditated plan of action to take one's own life.

Suicide: To take one's own life.

Trauma: An event or circumstance in which the individual perceives an immediate, physical threat to life. All physical, emotional, and mental resources are directed toward survival. The memory is not integrated as information but remains frozen with the original emotional distress intact. Often termed post-traumatic stress syndrome or post-traumatic stress disorder. Combat survivors, disaster survivors, and battered individuals display similar symptoms. Such symptoms include refusing to talk about the trauma. Additionally, hyper-vigilance, a hair-trigger startle response, and a mistrust of others that includes trustworthy loved ones, are displayed.

Undiagnosed depression: Mental health status of an individual who displays multiple symptoms of depression but remains undiagnosed and untreated.

Resources for Help

If you recognize the feelings and symptoms described in this book for yourself or your child and are looking for additional help, here is a partial list of national and international resources that specifically address intervention for adolescent depression, addiction, suicide prevention, and mental health.

Adolescent Transition
Oregon Social Learning Center
207 East Fourth Avenue Suite 202
Eugene, OR 97401
Phone: 541-485-2711
Web: http://www.oslc.org

African American Family Services
2616 Nicollett Avenue South
Minneapolis, Minnesota 55408
Phone: 612-871-7878
Fax: 612-871-2811
Web: http://www.aafs.net

American Foundation for Suicide Prevention (AFSP)
Bipolar Illness and Suicide
120 Wall Street, 22nd Floor
New York, New York 10005
Phone: 1-888-333-AFSP
Fax: 212-363-6237
E-mail: inquiry@afsp.org
Web: http://www.afsp.org

Latin American Youth Center
1419 Columbia Road, NW
Washington, DC 20009
Phone: 202-319-2225

Fax: 202-462-5696
E-mail: info@mail.layc-dc.org
Web: http://www.layc-dc.org

Minority Adolescent Drug Use Prevention
University of Houston
Houston, Texas 77204-5341
Phone: (713) 743-8555

National Adolescent Health Information Center
Division of Adolescent Medicine
Department of Pediatrics and Institute for Policy Studies
School of Medicine
University of California
San Francisco, California 94109
Phone: 415-502-4856

National Institute on Drug Abuse (NIDA)
6001 Executive Boulevard, Room 5213
Bethesda, MD 20892-9561
Phone: 301-443-1124
E-mail: information@nida.nih.gov
Web: http://www.nida.nih.gov

Pride Institute at Cornerstone
Gay, Lesbian, Bisexual Community
57 West 57th Street
New York, New York 10019
Phone: 800-54-PRIDE
E-mail: Support@pride-institute.com
Web: http://www.pride-institute.com

Reconnecting Youth
Psychosocial and Community Health Department
University of Washington
School of Nursing
Seattle, Washington 98195-7255
Teen Help

Phone: 800-291-5814
800-637-0701
Web: http://www.son.washington.edu/centers

Recovery Services, Inc.
965 Mission Street, Suite 325
San Francisco, California 94103
Phone: 415-541-9285
Fax: 415-541-9986
Web: http://www.aars-inc.org

Teens in Crisis
Worldwide Association of Specialty Programs and Schools
Phone: 800-398-7113

Society for Adolescent Medicine
1916 Copper Oaks Circle
Blue Springs, Missouri 64015
Phone: 816-224-8010
Fax: 816-224-8009
E-mail: Sam@adolescenthealth.org
Web: http://www.adolescenthealth.org

Students Against Destructive Decisions (National)
Box 800
Marlborough, Massachusetts 01752
Phone: 1-877-SADD-INC
Fax: 1-508-481-5759
Web: http://www.saddonline.com

Substance Abuse and Mental Health Services Administration
Center for Mental Health Services
Knowledge Exchange Network
PO Box 42557
Washington, DC 20015
Phone: 800-789-2647

TDD: 866-889-2647
Fax: 240-747-5470
Web: http://www.mentalhealth.org

United National Indian Tribal Youth, Inc.
UNITY
PO Box 800
Oklahoma City, Oklahoma 73101
Phone: 405-236-2800
Fax: 405-971-1071
Web: http://www.unityinc.org

Suggested Reading

Branden, Nathaniel. *The Disowned Self.* New York: Bantam Books, 1971.

Cammer, Leonard. *Up from Depression.* New York: Simon & Schuster, 1969.

Carter, Elizabeth A., and Monica McGoldrick, Ed. *The Family Life Cycle: A Framework for Family Therapy.* New York: Gardner Press, 1980.

Cobain, Bev. *When Nothing Matters Anymore: A Survival Guide for Depressed Teens.* Edited by Elizabeth Verdick. Minneapolis, MN: Free Spirit Publishing, 1998.

Fieve, Ronald R. *Moodswing.* New York: Simon & Schuster, 1975.

Giovacchini, Peter. *The Urge to Die: A Guide to Recognizing and Coping with Suicidal Behavior in Depressed Teens.* New York: Macmillan Publishing Co., 1981.

Gustavson, Cynthia Bloomquist. *In-Versing Your Life: A Poetry Book for Self Discovery and Healing.* Milwaukee, WI: Families International, 1995.

Hall, Calvin S., and G. Lindsey. *Theories of Personality.* New York: Wiley & Sons, 1978.

Hall, Calvin S., and Vernon J. Nordby. *A Primer of Jungian Psychology.* New York: New American Library, 1973.

Herman, Judith Lewis. *Trauma and Recovery.* New York: Basic Books, 1992.

Herr, Michael. *Dispatches.* New York: Vintage International, 1991.

Hopkins, Jerry, and D. Sugarman. *No One Gets Out of Here Alive.* New York: Warner Books, 1980.

Jamison, Kay Redfield. *Touched with Fire: Manic Depressive Illness and the Artistic Temperament.* New York: Simon & Schuster, 1993.

————. *An Unquiet Mind: A Memoir of Moods and Madness.* New York: Vintage Books, 1996.

————. *Night Falls Fast: Understanding Suicide.* New York: Vintage Books, 1999.

Jung, Carl. *The Portable Jung.* Edited by Joseph Campbell. New York: Penguin Books, 1971.

LeCroy, Craig Wilson, Ed. *Handbook of Child and Adolescent Treatment Manuals.* New York: Lexington Books, 1994.

Markova, Dawn. *I Will Not Die an Unlived Life: Reclaiming Purpose and Passion.* Berkeley, CA: Conari Press, 2000.

Miller, Jeffrey A. *The Childhood Depression Source Book.* Los Angeles: Lowell House, 1998.

Mosher, Jean W. *Life's Spectrum.* Milwaukee, WI: Jean Mosher Estate, 2002.

O'Brien, Tim. *The Things They Carried.* New York: Penguin Books, 1990.

National Institutes of Health. *Preventing Drug Use Among Children and Adolescents.* NIH Publication No 99-4212, 1997.

Pipher, Mary. *Reviving Ophelia: Saving the Selves of Adolescent Girls.* New York: Ball Ballantine Books, 1994.

Ratner, Ellen. *The Other Side of the Family: A Book for Recovery from Abuse, Incest and Neglect.* Deerfield Beach, FL: Health Communications Viscott, 1990.

Sander, Fred M. *Individual and Family Therapy: Towards an Integration.* New York: Jason Aronson, 1979.

Sholevar, G. PIrooz and L. Schwoeri, Ed. *The Transmission of Depression in Families: Assessment and Intervention.* Northvale, NJ: Jason Aronson, 1994.

Steinglass, Peter, L. A. Bennett, and Reiss Wolin. *The Alcoholic Family.* New York: Basic Books, 1987.

Viscott, David. *Risking.* New York: Pocket Books, 1977.

978-0-595-35993-6
0-595-35993-0